Our Economics
(IQTISADUNA)

OUR
ECONOMICS
(IQTISADUNA)

VOLUME I

A Critical Study Appraising the Economic Doctrines of
Marxism, Capitalism and Islam, Looking at Their
Ideological Foundations and Relevant Theories

BY

Muhammad Baqir Al-Sadr

Translation, Commentary, and General Editing
By
Dr Kadom Jawad Shubber

From the Arabic text 'Iqtisaduna'

Our Economics
(IQTISADUNA)

First Published in Great Britain, 2000
© BookExtra Ltd.

Published by

BookExtra
INTERNATIONAL PUBLISHERS & DISTRIBUTORS

P.O.Box: 12519
London, W9 1ZA, UK
Tel: (44) 020-7604 5523
Tel: (44) 020-7604 5508
Fax: (44) 020-7604 4921

E-mail:
sales@bookextra.com

Home Page:
www.bookextra.com

ISBN: 1 900560 07 0

In the name of Allah,
the Compassionate the
Merciful

Summary Contents
(Volumes I & II)

Contents of Volume I

Glossary

Capitalism: the economic system/doctrine, where private owners of capital are permitted the maximum degree of liberty to decide what is to be produced, where and how it is produced, in addition to associated consumer freedoms of purchase and utilisation.

Causality: principle that every event/ phenomenon/development has a cause (or a plurality of causes) which brings about the effect in question.

Class struggle: Marxist notion that different classes within society engage in conflict, owing to their varying interests and standpoints.

Communism: a socio-economic system where allegedly individuals would exert whatever efforts they are capable of, while enjoying whatever benefits/advantages they happen to require.

Complete (perfect) competition: a market set-up where embodying a large number of sellers, along with a large number of buyers, while the product/service is homogenous, and no traces of monopoly exist.

Consumer utility: degree of benefit/satisfaction derived from using a product or service, as perceived by the consumer.

Culture: the complete web of ascertainable patterns of social attitudes, behaviour and interactions among individuals, groups, and sections within a society, corporation, organisation etc.

Development strategy: the main thrust of the route to economic advancement, adopted by a nation/region to attain long and medium term economic objectives.

Dialectics: a philosophy which attempts to explain events and developments as resulting form conflicts, while assuming that he seeds of conflict are present within every development or phenomenon.

Economic dependency: the state whereby a nation's well-being - and possibly even livelihood - hinges substantially on the good-will and co-operation of a specific country or a set of countries.

Economic science: the social science dealing with issues pertaining to allocation of scare resources in order to cater for human needs at al levels of society.

Existentialism: a Western-based philosophy adhering to the view that no belief in anything can have proper validity unless it has practical existence in a materialistic and observable fashion, while stressing at same time the importance of personal experience and responsibility.

Feudalism: system of production built on the rabbles of slavery, whereby large landowners enjoy prime powers and wide-ranging influence.

Free-market economics: economic system/doctrine which advocates the minimum possible amount of State intervention in the national economy, thereby allowing people to mange their lives as they see fit.

Historical materialism: theory claiming that as the state of the production system(along with production forces) develop throughout history, the nature of the socio-economic system will change and adjust accordingly.

Iron law of wages: a theory expounded by certain classical Western-based economists, claiming that labour wages tended to remain at subsistence level, within the context of a freely functioning economy.

Islam: religion first declared by Prophet Muhammad in early 7th Century AD, and expounded by the Holy Quran, demeanour and sayings of the Prophet and his trusted companions and immediate members of his household.

Law of changing returns to scale: when all factors of production except one are held constant, and the quantity of this one factor is gradually increased form point zero, then at first we will experience increasing returns to scale (i.e. productivity of the controlled factor will be increasing), then decreasing returns and eventually negative returns may set in.

Law of overall limitation: total Earthly production - over a given period - of any item that utilises land and/or extracted raw materials is limited by the total quantity available of land and/or relevant materials that can be mined during that period.

Marxism: the doctrine, arguments and ideas presented by Karl Marx(1818-1883), along with his associates, relating to the interplay of economic forces, nature of production relationships in society, and evolution of socio-economic systems throughout human history.

Means of production: methods, conduits and tools used by people in order to produce various goods and services, within the context of prevailing knowledge and techniques.

Mercantilism: the economic philosophy which spread in the West during the 16th and 17th centuries, calling for managed trade among nations, and alleging that in trade the gain of one nation was the loss of another.

Monopoly: market situation where one producer (or a small group of producers acting in concert) dominate, either wholly or largely, the supply of a given product/service or a category of products/services, within a market that is global, national, regional, or local in scope and dimension.

Multiplier effect: augmented final outcome on the whole economy, resulting from an event/phenomenon (positive or negative), e.g. reduction in investment or rise in income for a group of people.

Natural freedom: room of manoeuvre enjoyed in a natural way by living organisms, including humans. The extent of this freedom, however, varies from one species to another.

Physiocracy: a major 18th century Western movement (concentrated in France) , which believed that the operation of any economy was governed by certain natural laws, and that those laws could be discovered. Proponents of this doctrine also believed that the only real output was agricultural production.

Planned economy: the system involving the periodic setting by the State of a general - or even detailed - framework for the conduct and outcome of economic activities over a future time period, e.g. five years.

Political economy: social science dealing with issues where the two fields of 'economics' and 'politics' interface.

Public ownership: wherever assets-especially of productive types - are owned by the State, on behalf of society as a whole.

Reformation: movement mainly in Europe during 16th century which called for enlightenment, dilution of the powers of the Church and even separation from Rome-based Catholicism.

Slavery: production system embodying wide-ranging employment of slave labour. According to proponents of the theory of historical materialism, this system followed that of primitive communism.

Social freedom: liberty enjoyed by human beings by virtue of the socio-political system in which they live.

Social production: where products/services are produced through group effort on the part of the labour force, rather than individual or special human input.

Socialism: the economic system where the State possesses the prime (materialistic) means of production, especially equipment, land and buildings.

Standard time: average time taken by an operative with average skill to produce one unit of product/service.

Synthesis: a Hegelian concept, asserting that every state of affairs (thesis) contains within it an element of opposition or contradiction (anti-thesis); the conflict between the two produces a compromise (synthesis).

Unemployment: the phenomenon where people are ready and able to work but cannot find suitable jobs.

Value added: difference between the market value of goods/services produced and the value of material inputs utilised in production, i.e. the former minus the latter.

Value in exchange: price that a product/service procures in the market, in terms of generally acceptable currency, or in exchange for other items.

Value in use: benefit obtained by customer from a product/service when actually utilised.

Publisher's Note

Some forty years have passed since the first Arabic edition of *Iqtisaduna* (Our Economics) saw the light of day. That classic book in the field of comparative political economy was the *second* major work to be published by the late Mohammad Baqir AL-Sadr, a Muslim cleric who took it upon himself to elucidate major ingredients of Islam that pertained to society's well-being and enlightenment, as well as to the understanding by ordinary Muslim individuals of the foundations of their beliefs and the path to attain better life, both in this world and the hereafter. The first major work produced by Al-Sadr was *Falsafatuna* (Our Philosophy)

A number of factors have combined to perpetuate *Iqtisaduna*, making it as relevant today as it was when first published. In fact, a case can be made out to show that it is now incumbent upon every individual who wishes to know something on political economy to study this text, in order to become acquainted with the main economic message of Islam in this field, along with relevant comparisons with socialism and free-market economics.

The past few decades have been rich with important events and developments, which have in the main supported the general ethos of this book and made it more relevant to today's world. Among such events and developments are the spectacular expansion of non-usurious banking and finance, the growth of pan-Islamic political movements, and the adoption of Islam as the political and socio-economic system of the State in countries such as Iran, Pakistan and Sudan.

The collapse of socialist regimes in the former Soviet Union and Eastern Europe has also made it more pressing for a viable *third way* to be present, clear and alive. While the models of socialism and communism are still with us in principle, a practical and credible alternative to capitalism is very much needed, particularly in the context of the Muslim world.

These and other developments raise vital issues relating to what dealings or practices are permitted by Islam in the various fields of commerce, production, services and investment. In addition, there are philosophical and moral considerations, as well as questions concerned with development, culture, economic growth and the distribution of wealth, that need to be thoroughly looked at.

The book addresses all these matters in a highly convincing and analytic manner. What is more is that Al-Sadr had had no formal training in economics, finance, philosophy or sociology, indicating therefore the amount of study that the author had to endure in order to produce the book. All this adds to the remarkable nature of this work, and makes it imperative that non-Arabic readers should have access to the concepts, analysis and sheer volume of knowledge that it embodies.

The book in your hands is not a mere translation of the Arabic text. No effort has been spared in attempting to mould the Arabic book in a modern, clear English-language volume on comparative political economy. The overriding objective has been to re-produce *Iqtisaduna* in a modern English version that is lucid, understandable and useful to all concerned.

Arabic and English are two great languages, rich with culture and accumulated heritage. As each has its particular style and mannerism, a literal translation could do much damage to *Iqtisaduna*. In consequence, it was necessary to consider fully the gist of every theory, idea, sentence, and even word, so as to re-express them in a meaningful, coherent, and succinct way to English readers.

Additional comments and notes have been included to bring the text to the standards of knowledge and presentation of the 21st century. In some cases, materials in the Arabic text have been expanded, while in other instances summarised. Where appropriate, footnote comments have been inserted, in order to provide relevant explanations, while in other cases footnote references have been added to authenticate the analysis and facilitate research in the respective areas.

Due to the sheer size of this work, the decision was taken to publish the book in two volumes. Volume I looks at Marxism and capitalism, containing thereby two main parts. Volume II is devoted to Islamic economics, and comprises four parts, in addition to the appendices. The contents in Volume II look in some detail at various aspects of Islamic economics, including such matters as distribution theory, the view towards natural resources, treatment of risk, nature of the exchange process, economic growth, and economic responsibility of the State.

Each of these two volumes contains a glossary of technical terms, a name-index and a subject-index. This information represents a further addition for the benefit of English-language readers that did not appear in the original Arabic text.

No pretences are made, however, that either of these two volumes is perfect or flawless, or that no criticism can be levelled against their contents or style. The publishers, along with the translator/editor are keen to receive all pertinent comments from interested readers and undertake to consider them for subsequent editions, with willingness and grace of the **Almighty Allah**.

Dr. Hassan Bashir
Managing Director of BookExtra

AUTHOR'S PREFACE
TO THE SECOND EDITION

In the name of Allah, the Merciful, the Compassionate

It pleases me greatly to present the second edition of **Iqtisaduna** (Our Economics). I have become more and more convinced that our society (the Muslim community) has actually begun to understand the true message that Islam represents, so much so that Islam *is* now viewed as the path to salvation, and that the Islamic system *is* the natural framework within which Muslims ought to plan and conduct their daily lives, in order to utilise their abilities and resources to the full.

I would have liked to have had the opportunity to expand on some topics of the book, so as to focus more intensively on a number of issues dealt within the pages of this work. While circumstances have not facilitated this, I would take this opportunity to comment on the subject-matter of the book, and its substantive and increasing impact on people's lives, not only in the context of the Muslim world, but also as pertaining to humanity in general.

Muslims are presently engaged in nothing less than a **holy war** against backwardness and deprivation. There is a clearly discernible renaissance, both politically and socially, towards a better existence, and a more solid economic structure, which provides for prosperity and welfare to all. And, after a string of trials and errors, Muslims will find that there is **only** one route along which to proceed - the path of Islam. The Islamic framework provides solutions to

problems   of economic backwardness, enabling individuals to
overcome their current intricate difficulties.

Humanity has been suffering in diverse ways, due to worries caused
by the nuclear arm race and the constant accumulation of awful
weaponry, as well as   gyrations between two immensely powerful
camps[1]. However,   a permanent opening continues to be available to
everyone, providing a much-needed deliverance. This is the Heavenly
gate of Islam, that remains ajar to all people on this planet,
irrespective of race, creed, colour, wealth, or any other consideration.

ISLAM AND THE WEST

When Muslims began to open up to Western civilisation (mainly
Western Europe)[2], Europeans wielded their intellectual, industrial,
and economic superiority - a phenomenon that convinced Muslims
to acquiesce to the supremacy of the European individual. This
helped to displace the erstwhile belief among Muslims in the real
message and original guidance rendered by their religion to all
mankind.

More seriously, Muslims began to comprehend their place within a
world divided between *poorer nations*, that were dependent and
subservient to other *advanced and prosperous* countries. As
Muslims generally lived and bred within the former group of
countries, they were viewed - and they regarded themselves - as

---

[1] The author wrote the book at a time when rivalry between the US-led NATO and the
Warsaw-Pact countries, dominated by the Soviet Union, was at its height, with great
consequences for Third World nations. It could perhaps be said that to a large extent, the
legacy of that situation is still with us today.

[2] The author refers to **Europe**, as indicating the **West**. This is understandable, as the occupying
powers in the Muslim world were mainly West European countries, mainly Britain, Italy,
France, Spain, Portugal, and Holland. Although the US is now the undisputed leader of the
West, the former is nothing but **'United Europe Overseas'**, in the words of Harold
Macmillan, an ex-British prime minister. Throughout, the word *Europe*(and *Europeans*) will
be used interchangeably with the *West*(and *Westerners*).

competence to issue directives and plan what was considered to be the *right route* for advancement.

From the outset, therefore, the Muslim world regarded itself as *economically inferior*, and perceived its major problem as one of economic underdevelopment-cum-backwardness vis-à-vis the more developed and industrialised west, which assumed world leadership by virtue of economic advancement.

Moreover, the developed countries of the West indicated to Muslims that virtually the only path for progress and economic development was to adopt Western life-styles, and the European individual had to be viewed as a *model,* that needed to be emulated. Only through such a strategy- Muslims were led to believe - could a vibrant and modern economic structure be built, so that Muslim nations might overcome their economic ills and aspire to stand on par with modern European nations.

In consequence, three chronological yet different patterns can be identified, to express the subordination of Muslim nations towards European countries, which spearheaded modern civilisation. These three patterns remain concurrent today, though in different parts of the Muslim world, while the relative importance of each has been changing:

First: *political subordination*, which had been expressed through direct rule of the less developed nations.

Second: *economic dependency*, which came about when the erstwhile colonies gained political independence, while Western countries (and their corporations) were given ample scope to invest and market their products, in those regions. All this enabled the developed West (through its powerful corporations) to be the prime investors in the natural-resource sectors of many Muslim countries, while in many cases foreign-owned businesses acquired total or relative monopoly positions within the economies of the poorer nations. The rationale which was put forward to explain this was the need to **train** the indigenous population, who were not yet ready to shoulder the tasks of economically developing heir homeland.

Third: *dependency of development strategy*, adopted by Muslim nations. Many experiments had been embarked upon in order to break free from the cycle of economic backwardness and Western domination, but virtually none of these attempts came to fruition. This was primarily due to the mental framework that limited thinking within the Western-imposed mould. In consequence, many leaders of Muslim nations could not engage in the lateral thinking necessary to truly understand their nations' socio-economic problems within the context of their own societies.

As a result, the various development approaches pursued by Muslim countries had a common thread, in that they were all based on the modern experiences of Europeans, and did not deviate radically from that general pattern. In essence, therefore, attempts by Muslim countries to construct a modern thriving economy have fallen between two prime models that Europeans had previously experienced, i.e. the *free-market* model and the *planned-economy* model.

However, it needs to be recognised that when either of these two models was applied by Muslims, certain *adjustments* were made to take local conditions into consideration. It is also necessary to note that free-market economics had *precedence*, in the sense that it was first to permeate Muslim societies, due to the fact that such concepts found their way to the Muslim world prior to the rival socialist model.

It is also true to say that experiments with socialism were - for the most part - a *reaction* to Western political domination. In other words, socialism was regarded as the *anti-thesis* of capitalism, and as the latter was associated with the excesses and manifestations of colonial rule, it was regarded as proper to move to the other side as a strategy to attain social and economic development. It is, however, important to recognise that the adoption of some form of a planned economy did **not** contravene the attitudinal assumption that Europeans were superior, and that experiments in this area had to be within broad guidelines set out by this assumption.

Proponents of each model-capitalism and socialism - had their own arguments and rationale to underpin their viewpoint. In the case of capitalism, the great strides accomplished by Western societies that adhered to that model can be quoted as evidence of success. This same path - the argument runs - can furnish the opportunity to under-developed nations to follow suit, thereby saving time and effort, in order to reach objectives, through benefiting from the experiences, technologies and scientific achievements, which were attained only via constant efforts by the West over centuries.

The arguments presented by the socialist camp emphasise that what proved to be instrumental and successful for Western Europe need not be so for the poorer nations of the developed world of our times. Today's poorer nations face huge economic challenges that can not be tackled through a pragmatic, piecemeal and experimental approach. They stress that present circumstances require underdeveloped nations to mobilise all their resources - human and otherwise - in the development process, and within the framework of a clear and well-focused strategy, so as to achieve high rates of growth, by shunning wastage and unproductive pursuits, while avoiding the luxuries embodied in a trial and error strategy.

It is pertinent to note that the supporters of either camp are eager to bring out the practical pitfalls of the other approach, in order to underpin their viewpoint. In this process, they take the often miserable conditions of previously colonised societies as the starting point of contention. Yet, both camps tend invariably to ignore the existence of at least a theoretical **third model**, provided by Islam and the economic system inherent therein.

REQUIRED COMPARISON

At this juncture, I do not wish to compare Islamic economics, on the one hand, with free-market and socialist economics, on the other. The rest of the book will take care of this task.

However, I do want here to refer to the appropriateness of these two diametrically opposed models, in the context of their relevance to the struggle of Muslim countries to rid themselves of economic backwardness and dependency, and the suitability of each to be an effective framework and basis for socio-economic development. The two main models in this regard are *Islamic economics*, on the one hand, and *European economics* (both capitalist and socialist), on the other.

Let us now set aside the ideological comparison among the different economic doctrines, and look at the *appropriateness* of each to provide a conducive development framework. Here, we need to consider the relevant conditions and practical parameters within each society, including pertinent psychic make-up and history.

This implies, quite clearly, that the practical usefulness of capitalism or socialism for Europeans need not hold true for other cultures. An economic system is a major component of an integrated whole, which is the society at large, that has come into being though historical progression, influenced greatly by such philosophies and events as religion, wars, famines, geography etc. Thus, an economic system separated from its relevant cultural environment may *not* be as effective to deliver the expected results.

It is therefore necessary to realise that choosing an economic system is not a task that a State, or a government, can undertake *without* enlisting the full understanding and true conviction of ordinary individuals. The nature of the intricate battle against backwardness makes it imperative that any economic system selected must resonate and integrate effectively with other cultural components of the wider society, as this will be a basic requirement for the success of the development effort. All this is needed for overcoming backwardness, and enabling the whole society to grow both externally and internally, in a coherent and well co-ordinated fashion.

The experience of Europeans is a clear historical expression of this fact. The practical success of European economies over the past few centuries would *not* have been possible without the full participation of European nations themselves, and their psychological and social involvement in this process, in all walks of endeavour.

It is therefore obvious that when a development strategy is to be chosen for the Muslim world, this fact must be *fully* recognised. We need to search for a cultural vehicle which is relevant and capable to mobilise the people, enlisting in the process their knowledge and energies in the great battle against backwardness. The feelings and inclinations of ordinary people will need to be taken into consideration, along with all relevant historical and emotional ramifications.

There are, for instance, deep suspicions across the Muslim world towards the erstwhile colonial powers, mixed with various accusations and fears, which have been the consequence of a long history of exploitation and struggle. All this has spawned *apprehensions* and *concerns* among Muslims towards all systems and concepts that are derived from the organisational or cultural parameters of European countries.

Such sensitivities have made Western-inspired economic recipes unwelcome in the Muslim world, even in situations where they might otherwise have been practical and conducive to effective economic development. It is quite possible that had those economic doctrines been separated from colonialism and its political overtones, they *could* have proved instrumental in engendering worthwhile development within Muslim societies.

All this may explain the viewpoint assumed by some political groupings in the Muslim world, which have leaned towards

nationalism. In large measure, this has been prompted by the necessity to formulate philosophies and hoist slogans that are wholly different from colonialism. Yet, nationalism is nothing but a historical and linguistic bond. By its nature, it is neutral, and does **not** furnish any coherent philosophy for life and the universe.

All this has prompted many nationalistic movements within the Muslim world to adopt certain doctrines and specific social systems, attempting in the process to accommodate this with their original banners, which were viewed as independent form the European message. Hence the adoption of socialism by pan-Arab political movements, which have embraced the notion of *'Arab socialism'*. This attempt should, in general, be seen as a failure, because socialism is again alien to the realm of Islam and to the Muslim world.

This unwholesome element represented by socialism has not passed unnoticed in the Arab world, as social and emotional conditions do not provide an encouraging backdrop for such a system. Proponents of Arab socialism have been **unable** to present any novel element in this 'socialism', and have in fact implicitly admitted as much through attempting to cloak it with an **Arab** colour. For they must know - before anybody else - that the Arab nation is highly sensitive to anything that smacks of a link with the colonial era, with the endeavour being directly primarily towards building a modern structure based on truly indigenous foundations.

A basic ingredient that must therefore be present, in any politico-economic approach or philosophy, for progress and development of Arab and Muslim nations, is the requirement to recognise **our** heritage, past glories, and the true essence of our religion-Islam. Any doctrines that have the stamp of ex-colonialists are doomed to failure, while any approaches having key elements pertaining to our culture and glorious past will possess a high probability of success in the continuing battle to rid Muslim societies of poverty and backwardness.

Another factor which ties in with the above reasoning is the fact that Western economic thinking **contradicts** the religious beliefs and attitudes of Muslims[3]. In this context, I am not comparing Western and Islamic economic thinking, so as to show that one is preferable to the other. I am merely stating that despite attempts by the Western powers, which occupied or influenced the Muslim world in the past, seeking in the process to implant Western values, culture, and way of thinking, Muslims have managed to preserve mush of their traditional life-style, feelings, behaviour, and viewpoints.

An Islamic-oriented development strategy will therefore **not** face the resistance and complications that are likely to dog any alien economic philosophy. In fact, a culture-friendly development doctrine will be significantly assisted by widely-held religious beliefs, due to the generally deep-seated faith among Muslims in the righteousness of their religion, and that Islam is a religion ordained by the Heavens through the last Messenger, Mohammed (Peace be Upon Him).

When looking at the West and the Muslim world, we find two **distinct** cultures, which influence greatly individual behaviour and generally-acceptable mannerism. Undoubtedly, Western culture has been supportive to economic, social, political and technological progress in Western countries, yet that culture is clearly **at odds** with Muslim societies.

It would be **fallacious** to argue that fertile ground would be cultivated, for Western-inclined economic thinking in the Muslim world, through weakening religious beliefs among Muslims. For one thing, **how long** would it take for such a process to be implemented? Also, what **means** ought to be utilised, and to what **extent** would the process be successful? And, when faith is destroyed or made ineffective/dormant, what is it **replaced** by?

---

[3] For instance, many Muslims continue to refrain from drinking alcohol or indulging in gambling, even where such acts are permitted by prevailing politico-social systems.

The plain fact is that Islamic culture is so **entrenched** within Muslim societies, that any attempts at weakening or dilution cannot hope to be more than partially successful. Any strategies, or plans, to overcome backwardness **must** consequently take cognisance of the nature of the respective society, including the current value system, as well as the degree of understanding and co-operation between ordinary individuals, on the one hand, and those who plot strategy and put together plans, on the other hand.

WESTERN CULTURE

This brings us to a **profound** distinction between Western and Muslim cultures. Westerners have always looked to the Earth they stand on, rather to the Heavens, in evolving their outlook and viewpoints. The fact that Christianity has spread throughout the West has not changed this, as Westerners have brought down their faith to an Earthly level, instead of uplifting their beliefs to the Heavens. There is no clearer symbolism of this than the attempt to bring down a God to Earth to show Him as a human being, instead of believing in an abstract unseen God.

There are also the attempts to search for **linkages** between humans and other animal species, endeavouring to explain humanity through the process of adaptation to land and environment. All that is inextricably related with attempts to understand human attitudes and behaviours within the context of the interplay of productive powers in society.

Those lines of thinking have enabled Westerners to evolve **specific values**, pertaining to wealth, ownership and materialism, that have been solidified and polished throughout history, so as to produce such concepts as lust and self-interest, which dominate both thinking and behaviour in the West today. The West's basic values, and derivative concepts, have played a pivotal role in tapping energies of individuals, as well as in the formulation of specific and effective targets and strategies for advancement, resulting thereby in accomplishing the requisite integration to produce an never-ending momentum for material betterment.

In addition, the virtual *separation* of the Western individual from the Almighty, and the focus of the former on Earth in lieu of the Heavens, has deprived that individual from any realistic notions embodying the supremacy of a higher power. Nor do Westerners, in general, recognise any constraints imposed on them from outside their own framework, a fact that has prepared them mentally and emotionally to believe in their liberty, resulting logically in an extended feeling of independence and individualism.

All the above has been translated into the philosophy of **existentialism**, which can without doubt be viewed as one of the great philosophical tendencies of the West. The intertwined concepts of liberty and individualism have contributed substantially to the success of free-market economies as well as planned economies in Europe, as concepts associated with individualism and self-interest remained of a paramount importance. In cases where planned economics (or socialism) gained the upper hand, pure materialistic individualism and self-interest were transformed into their equivalent notions on the social class level[4].

All in all, the notion of **liberty** had become the channel for the evolution and development of another primary concept in the European psyche, i.e. the idea of **struggle**. This latter concept made Europeans endeavour to reach out for any goal that they envisaged, however challenging. But they always felt constrained by the *other* individual, who may stand on the other side, and hence the attempts to cancel the other person became part and parcel of the European frame of mind.

It is clear that this concept of *struggle* has become a central element of modern Western philosophy and culture, and there are important manifestations of this in the legal, social, political and economic

---

[4] It is perhaps arguable whether this transformation has been effected in a total or partial manner

fields. The struggle for survival has become a basic dogma, whether in the world of nature (i.e. among living creatures), or among social classes within a given society. Other consequences of the notion of struggle are the phenomena of *dialectics*, and the reliance on thesis, antithesis and synthesis to develop new notions and to explain developments in history, science and theoretical formulation.

The concept of struggle has also been amply manifested via individual and business **rivalry**.   Countless examples exist of the sharp methods used by Western businesses in competing with on another, while instances of such tactics are no less severe in cases of individual rivalry.   On the level of group action (such as labour unions and professional bodes), examples of struggle and competition similarly abound.   Al this has made it *possible* to attain progress and economic development, on all levels of society, starting from the single individual to the community in general.

ISLAMIC CULTURE

In contrast to all the above, there is the culture and patterns of behaviour that are prevalent within the **Muslim world**. By nature, the Eastern individual looks to the *Heavens* prior to looking at Earth, due to the chronology of history and the impact of upbringing, with much reverence toward metaphysics, *rather* than the material and what is directly noticeable.

This keen interest in **metaphysics** has been expressed eloquently in the life of Muslims. They have paid great attention to the *cognitive* aspects of life, as distinct from what can be directly ascertained, resulting logically and surely in a relatively limited pre-occupation with material objects.

All this has brought about some special *standpoints* vis-à-vis materialism, among which is excessive modesty, or being satisfied with only the basic requirements of material possessions. To be sure, laziness may be viewed as a third manifestation of this indifference towards materialism.

Consequently, pious Muslims have become accustomed to feeling the presence of *invisible* monitoring. As a result, good Muslims feel innately responsible to God in all their thought and actions, and this places significant limitations on their personal freedom, in ways that do not exist in the case of a Western individual. A corollary of this is that a Muslim feels a strong bond towards the ***group*** and senses the need to consider the collective interest of his/her group, while in contrast a modern Westerner tends to be obsessed with the concept of struggle.

A major factor that has underpinned this **'collective'** concept is the nature of Islam's world-wide message to all humanity, and the requirement for all Muslims to spread their religion and make adherents of other faiths aware of what God has ordained in the Holy Quran. Such an emphasis on collectivity and the common good - on the local, regional and global levels - has some important bearings on the type of economic system that Islam calls for. And the ***integration*** between culture and economics in Islam will assist in attaining progress and development, just as such intertwining has been so strongly instrumental and beneficial in the West.

Within the context of an Islamic society, work will be a **duty**, and dealing with Earthly matters will be within the confines of a Heavenly connotation, thus resulting in high energy and strong momentum to accomplish development and economic progress. Feelings of apathy and detachment presently experienced by Muslims towards Earthly values will vanish. Other negative psychic states, which are likely to disappear as well, are worries resulting when active Muslims work in the service of a free-market economic or a centrally-planned system. And this does not hold true only for devout and practising Muslims, but also non-practising individuals who know deep down that they are acting as a component in a wheel that is not of their choosing.

In addition, an individual living in an Islamic society will be better able to *tackle* many of the difficulties that flow from the operation of a free-market economy. Also, the act of belonging, and the consequent bond with a group, will contribute to the cultivation of capabilities and mobilisation of energies within society, in the context of overcoming backwardness. This would be especially fitting, if the battle for development was packaged and directed astutely, to give it the aura of a **holy war** to preserve the cohesion of the Muslim society, and sustain it on the path of the Holy Quran, as Allah(God) says:

'And prepare for them all that you can of strength and power...'

It is clear here that **power** in this context includes economic strength, as symbolised by the volume and standard of output produced by society. There is no doubt that this output is a major instrument in society's battle and the ever-continuing endeavour to protect its cultural values and sovereignty.

And, herein lies the paramount importance of **Islamic economics**, as a system which helps to preserve the true and indigenous culture of the Muslim world, as well as utilising relevant modes of individual behaviour in the process of economic construction.

It is pertinent to note that some Western writers have come to understand this fact, and have admitted that their value system and development programmes may *not* suit the Muslim world. However, I do wish to emphasise here that the attention given by Muslims toward the Heavens does *not* indicate that they are resigned to fate, awaiting whatever comes, and feeling helpless. This is the impression conveyed by some Western writers.

The true orientation of Muslims in this regard is amply described by the notion that a human being is the **vicegerent** of God on Earth. This notion illustrates in a rich and powerful fashion the ability of the human race to utilise all their energies and capabilities to exploit and develop the wealth and diversity that they find on Earth. Also, being a vicegerent is far *removed* from being subject to fate, as the first embodies a responsibility towards the Master, which entails - by definition - adequate authority to do as one thinks fit.

In addition, *adopting* Islam as a system for the whole community will allow individuals to structure all aspects of their lives on a uniform basis, especially from the spiritual and social angels. Islam extends to *all* aspects of life, while certain other systems and/or philosophies are restricted in scope to cover social and/or economic aspects only. If we Muslims build aspects of our daily life - say social or economic or both - on the basis of something other than Islam, we would need grounding for the spiritual side. As we have *nothing* other than Islam to cater for our spiritual well-being, a contradiction would ensue between the spiritual and worldly sides of life. The inevitable conclusion, therefore, is that we need to construct the various major elements of our living within the **Islamic framework,** owing to the deep and intricate interfacing of these elements, especially those pertaining to spiritual, economic and social aspects.

AUTHOR'S PREFACE
TO THE FIRST EDITION

In the name of Allah, the Merciful, the Compassionate

A promise was made at the end of my book **'Our Philosophy'** (*Falsafatuna*)[1] to continue the series of high-level Islamic studies. That work (i.e. *Falsafatuna*) was the first within a line of books, tackling basic Islamic concepts, to be followed by others that deal with additional or extended aspects within the great Islamic edifice. The objective is to put together the co-ordinated elements of Islamic thinking, as a complete and integrated approach to life, that will remain alive within our conscience.

In my original plan, the second major book would have be **'Our Society'** (*Mujtamauna*), but this work was postponed, due to persistent demands from readers, who have unceasingly suggested the need for a volume to look at economic issues from an Islamic perspective. In fact, I was aiming for this work to be finalised before this day, but certain unforeseen circumstances led to some delay, despite, the exceptional efforts and assistance rendered by my devout colleague, the reverable scholar Sayeed Mohammad Baqir AL-Hakim.

---

[1] *Falsafatuna* was the first major work published by the author, setting the basic tenets of Islamic thinking in the area of philosophy, and exploring Islam's general view to the universe and life.

It is important here to make a distinction between the **science of economics** and **economic doctrine**[2]. **Economic science** is a field of study attempting to explain economic phenomena and events, through linking these with specific factors or reasons that determine the former[3]. Economic science is fairly recent, having been born - in the true meaning of the word - when the era of capitalism began, over four centuries ago, despite the fact that the primary roots of economic thinking can be traced deep into history.

Each civilisation had participated, to some degree, in thinking through economic issues, to the extent that resources and capabilities had been available to it. Yet, the fairly precise formats of theories presented by political economics are relatively new, and must be regarded as the outcome of research over mainly the last few centuries.

The **economic doctrine** of a given community (or a nation) can be regarded as the general vision or perspective through which that society views economic life, and how poignant problems may in practice be tackled. Viewed through such a perspective, no coherent society can be devoid of an economic doctrine or philosophy. Within each community, wealth has to be produced, preserved and distributed, and a methodology must exist for conducting these pivotal economic transactions. And, it is society's economic philosophy that **determines** the methods chosen to arrive at these decisions.

There is no doubt that **selecting** an economic philosophy for a given society is not a decision that is made lightly, but will always depend

---

[2] The author refers here to **positive economics** (economic science) and **normative economics** (economic philosophy/doctrine). The former contains a set of theories and analytic techniques within the contexts of presumptions made, while the latter pertains to the provision of advice to solve specific economic problems. See in this regard the following :
B T Allen : ' Managerial Economics' Harper & Row, 1988, Page 4
[3] For instance, economic science attempts to explain how prices of products or services are determined through the operation of supply and demand, within the context of a free-market economy. Another example, is the determination of wage and salary levels for different occupations/skills within the same context.

on certain basic notions that relate culture, history and experience. These fundamental concepts make up the ideological repository of any society's economic philosophy.

As a result, when we study a given economic philosophy, we need to analyse *two* important aspects, these being:

a) **general methodology** for organising economic life, including the setting of prices and pay levels, as well as the determination of products/services to be produced and their respective quantities.

b) **main repository** of concepts that are inter-linked with the economic philosophy, such as whether to allow certain types of products/services to be produced (e.g. alcoholic items).

When we study capitalism, for instance, we find it is based on the axiom of *economic liberty*, and thus it is necessary to consider the concepts on which this fundamental principle is based. Likewise, a similar consideration of the main and associated notions is warranted if we study other economic philosophies.

A case in point is the economic thought of the **mercantlists**, who believed - among other things - that any nation's wealth could be measured by the amount of precious metals possessed by them[4]. They called for managed trade, and the intervention of the State in the economy, believing that exports should be maximised and imports minimised, in order to attract as much money as possible into the country. All this contributed towards developing an economic philosophy that came to be called *mercantilism*, with consequent recipes for economic policy.

---

[4] *Mercantilism* had its golden age in the West during the period 1500 to 1750. That epoch was characterised by the decline of the manor (large landowners) and the rise of the nation-state. The main mercantilist economic theory was put forward by merchant businessmen, who assumed that in trade the gain of one nation was the loss of another. See in this regard the following work :
H Landreth & D C Colander: 'History of Economic Thought' 3rd edition, Houghton Mifflin Company, 1994, Pp 37-42.

Another example is the theory put forward by **physiocrats**, who thought that the only real output was agricultural production, and that this was the only means to augment wealth and add new value in society. In their view, trade and manufacturing were peripheral activities, claiming that free competition led to the best price. They added that society would benefit if individuals followed their self-interest, and that the burden of taxes had to fall on land, because the latter was the only real source of wealth[5].

Also, when **Thomas Malthus** presented his thesis on the population, he intended to guide policy-makers, so that the welfare of society could allegedly be served. He attempted to prove that population tended to increase at a faster rate than the food supply, and hence checks on population growth were necessary[6].

The theory put forward by Malthus has been amply criticised by economists, and has in fact been proven to be *inaccurate*. But during that epoch, the theory was relied upon by classical economists to support the so-called **'iron law of wages'**, which claimed that labour wages tended to remain at the subsistence level. Otherwise, high wages - as some governments were advocating at that time - would result in higher birth rates, which would create problems due to the insufficiency of food production[7].

When **socialists** put forward their theory to explain the **value** of any product, via the amount of work expended on it, this led them to the view that capitalist profits were repugnant. They also adopted the socialist notion in the distribution of wealth and income, which

---

[5] The physiocracy movement developed during the middle of the 18th century, and was concentrated in France. Physiocrats believed that natural laws governed the operation of any economy, and that these laws could be discovered. They focused on the real forces leading to economic development, and their thinking influenced Adam Smith, the Scottish economist who is frequently viewed as the father of classical (free-market) economic theory. See H Landreth & D C Colander, Op Cit, Pages 50-56

[6] The English economist *Thomas Robert Malthus* wrote seven essays on the population in the final years of the 18th century. Classical economists relied on the Malthusian theory to advocate keeping labour wage at low levels, in order to discourage larger families.

[7] For a discussion on Malthusian theory, see the following work:
H Landreth & D C Colander, Op. Cit., Pp 100-103.

entailed the inference that the worker was the rightful owner of all output, as his/her effort was - in their view - the only cause to create value.

For Karl Marx, the theory of **historical materialism** furnished the rock on which his economic doctrine was founded. In that theory, Marx claimed to have found the natural laws that determine the process of history, and concluded that his economic philosophy was the logical product of that theory. He thus regarded the inevitability of **socialism and communism** as flowing in the ordinary course of things from the theory of historical materialism.

In the case of **Islamic economics**, this is simply the economic doctrine founded on Islamic principles. It embodies the Islamic way of conducting economic affairs, based on pertinent accumulated ideology, which includes relevant concepts, culture and historical developments.

In this context, numerous questions may require answers. These include the viewpoint of Islam in determining values of various items (i.e. products and services), and the method through which any specific value is fixed. Also, is this value derived from labour alone, or from something else?

Again, we may need to know the Islamic viewpoint towards the role of capital and other factors of production. Here, it is necessary to look at the rights endowed by Islam on each of these elements within the system of distribution, as detailed in edicts relating to *Ijara* (leasing), *mudaraba* (speculation), *qardh* (lending), and other types of economic and financial transactions.

What remains of this book is split into seven main components. Parts I and II look respectively at Marxist and free-market economics, while Part III begins the process of exploring the economic doctrine of Islam by elucidating certain prime notions. Parts IV, V and VI deal with other more detailed aspects of Islamic economics, focusing mainly on the distribution system and production theory. The last part of the book contains appendices that relate to several specialised topics.

It is worthy to note at this juncture that the Islamic viewpoints expressed in the book are expounded *without* necessarily proving their logical derivation. In some cases, these views are supported by verses from the **Quran** or sayings from the **Prophet** (PBUH) etc., but this is generally *not* intended as a scientific proof in the full and proper sense. Also, the book contains views of various schools of thought in Islam, some of which *may not* fully or necessarily accord with the opinions held by the author.

It is proper to note that the main focus of the book is on general verdicts or standpoints regarding various issues, without delving on detailed intricacies. Moreover, the author has utilised certain terminologies and classifications that can not be easily found in books on Islamic jurisprudence. However, in all cases, such idioms are defined and explained within the text, while all categorisations presented are based essentially on Islamic law (Sharia).

The book does not cover merely the exterior surface of Islamic economics, nor is it pre-occupied primarily with rhetoric. In essence, this book's task is to penetrate deep into the **economic ideology of Islam**, so as to re-shape the relevant ideas into a proper mould, which facilitates the construction of a coherent structure of Islamic economics, that is rich in philosophy and ideas, clear in general nature and basic features, specific in the ways it interfaces with other economic doctrines, yet firmly embedded to the main body of Islam. Finally, I need to emphasise that the book must be viewed and read as a seedling for building edifice of Islamic economics, and providing the proper rationalisation for this field.

'And any good deeds that I have been able to attain are surely owing to the grace and guidance of Allah, on Whom I depend and to Whom I resort in all circumstances'.

Part I

Marxist Economics

Chapter 1:
Theory of Historical Materialism

Chapter 2:
Philosophical Foundations of Marxism

Chapter 3:
General Framework of Marxist Thought

Chapter 4:
Detailed Aspects of Marxist Economics

Chapter 5:
Socialism and Communism

~ *Chapter One* ~

Theory of Historical Materialism

The theory of **historical materialism** (*or* the 'material notion of history') is quite evidently *inseparable* from **Marxism** and the economic system embodied within the latter. According to Marx, that theory contains the *scientific laws* which cause events and developments to unfold.

The clear implication of this is that Marxism *will* become applicable at a certain stage, in the course of the natural historical progression of any given society. This natural progression of history determines – according to Marxism – the socio-economic **doctrine** that will predominate at any given stage in the course of any society's progress.

It follows logically from such a reasoning, that no socio-economic philosophy will prevail at a stage that is *not* synchronised with it, indicating quite clearly that the socio-economic make-up of any community and its corresponding state of development will *influence greatly* the general line of thinking at the time. By the same token, the theory (and Marxism as well) would reject out of hand the idea that any specific doctrine (e.g. Islam) could widely be held as a socio-economic system at different stages in a society's development and progression.

This is amply clarified by Friedrich Engels who states that:

"The conditions under which men produce and exchange vary from country to country, and within each country again from generation to generation. Political economy, therefore, cannot be the same for all countries and for all historical epochs".[1]

It is also clear that if the theory of historical materialism *fails* in performing its assigned role, then Marxism *disintegrates* as well. Historical materialism *would* fail if the type of socio-economic philosophy prevailing at any given phase does not correspond with that society's state of development, and also when people continue to hold the same philosophy irrespective of changes in the society's main structural framework.

1.1   SINGLE FACTOR THEORY

Historical materialism can be viewed as a **single-factor** theory to explain historical development, i.e. it focuses on *one* variable that decides the pattern of history. This theory is not alone in adopting such an approach, as many other writers and thinkers have chosen a similar path, in selecting simply one parameter and regarding it as the key to solve mysteries and explain the process of historical change. At best, these single-factor writers would not accorded other parameters more than an ancillary role in influencing events.

A case in point is the theory that *race* is the primary factor which determines the level of advancement of any community, influencing in the process the amount of wealth possessed by society, as well as the latent energies for innovation and progress. As the theory goes, the pure unadulterated human race is the prime mover of all forms of life in society, from the beginning of time to the present. It is also the essential ingredient that makes up humans, both physically and

---

[1] Friedrich Engels: "Herr Eugen Duhring's Revolution in Science (*Anti-Duhring*)" Lawrence & Wishart, London, Pg. 167 (no date given).

emotionally. The result is that history is nothing but an inter-connected series of rivalry and struggles among the various races, where the strong and pure will be victorious, while small insignificant nations wither away and vanish.

Another single-factor theory of history is based on **geography**. The claim here is that the history of different nations is influenced primarily by geographical and natural phenomena. This parameter is the one which provides – according to the theory – a nation with the means for advancement and sophisticated culture, awakening creative ideas in the minds of individuals. And conversely, it may play a critical role in inhibiting creativity, holding a community behind at the bottom of the ladder, in terms of scientific progress, wealth, power, and rate of economic growth.

Focusing on **sexual** desires is yet a third single-variable theory that some have advocated. Proponents of this theory – who have often been psychologists – have regarded this factor as highly instrumental in directing various human activities, influencing thereby the movement of history and the general shape of society.

Thus the theory of historical materialism can be viewed in the **same light**, as another single-factor endeavour to explain history. Karl Marx believed in it strongly, emphasising the role of the economic factor as the most significant determinant on the formation of society and its structure. Any other variables will only have peripheral influences, and – in any case – these other factors will largely adapt and change in tune with economic forces.

It must be said, quite plainly, that all the above theories accord with **neither** fact **nor** the teachings of Islam. Each of these single-variable theories has attempted to bundle all major influences on human life in one simple explanation, giving to this single variable more credit than it deserves, when we consider fully any phenomena and/or development.

1.2   THE ECONOMIC FACTOR

Marxism, therefore, views the economic factor as *the* determinant of any society's general circumstances, in the fields of politics, sociology, religion, ideology, as well as other aspects.   In turn, the economic situation is shaped by any society's **productive forces** and corresponding means of production.

In essence, Marxism regards the means (or factors) of production as *greatest* power in society, that moulds history and directs development and patterns of organisation.   Two major *issues* arise in this connection, and each requires a plausible response from Marxist ideology.   These two issues are:

A) what are the **means of production**?
B) how is **historical development** affected by these means?

The Marxist response to the first question is that the *forces (means) of production* symbolise the methods, conduits or tools used by people, in order to produce their requirements.   Since the beginning of time, humans have employed their own hands and physical strength, then tools began to used (e.g. rocks, hammers, knives, axes), and development continued till the present, whereby sophisticated machines, computers, robots, atoms and other power-driven apparatuses are put to great advantage in various processes of production.

With regard to the second question, Marxist thinking asserts that the progress, development, and contradictions of those forces of production (and corresponding technology) result in *significant historical changes*.   The forces of production *change* continually, and these changes will affect the nature of production relationships among people.   In all circumstances, and under whatever conditions, production involves the weaving of human links among people.

Production relationships are in fact intertwined with the issue of **ownership**, which is a critical element in the overall economic structure of society. Indeed, Marx believed that property relationships shape and determine the relationships of production, and consequently the distribution of wealth in society, and the type of ownership that is prevalent within it (e.g. slavery, feudalistic, capitalistic, socialist).

In essence, therefore, Marx did *not* distinguish between the relationships of production and property relationships, regarding the two as one and the same thing. What is more, he viewed the set-up of these relationships as the foundations over which the upper structure of society (e.g. political institutions, legal framework) is put together.

The next pertinent issue that comes to the surface is this: how does these production/ownership relationships *come about*? The Marxist answer to this crucial question is that the pattern of production and the state of production forces are the relevant **determinants** of production/ownership relationships. The clear implication of this is that each type of production system (e.g. feudalistic or capitalistic) is coupled with a pertinent set of production/property relations.

The Marxist view is that it is the state of the productive forces that *shapes* the general economic scene, along with its embodiments of property relations, social structure, legal system, and so on. A society's economic set-up would continue unaltered, until the productive forces reach a distinctly new stage in their maturity and development, which would entail a markedly new economic system with all its associated ramifications.

Each socio-economic system would not, however, come about easily and without pain. Historical materialism, which is an integral part of Marxism, necessitates that a **struggle** takes place between the productive forces and the out-dated system, so that a new socio-economic system is evolved. This is the essential nature of the dialectic process, where:

An antithesis (e.g. newly developed/evolved production forces) dispute the prevailing socio-economic system (thesis), and a compromise in the form of a different system (synthesis) comes about.

Herein lies the importance and role of the **class struggle**. Marx essentially saw a struggle between *two* main sections within society. The first comprises all those whose interest tie in with the new developed state of the productive forces, while members of the other section side with the *status quo*, i.e. preservation of prevailing production/ownership relations. This leads to contradiction and struggles, which Marx believed will result in the productive forces occupying the higher ground, whereby a different socio-economic system is evolved.

A society which is in a state of flux would, therefore, experience and exhibit two types of *conflict* and consequent clashes:

A)   **contradictions** between developing production forces and ruling property/production relationships.

B)   **struggle** between a social class allied to the productive forces, and another with vested interests in keeping the *status quo*. This conflict is the social expression of the first struggle, reflecting its multi-various dimensions.

As the forces of production are the more *crucial* within the fabric of society, and in effecting the production of the multitude of goods and services necessitated by people, it is imperative that the productive forces will gain the **upper hand**. Economic states that have become out-dated and disadvantageous to the productive forces will be rectified.

In social terms, this implies that the social classes that sided *with* the productive forces will be winners, resulting thereby in the destruction of the old production/ownership set-up. The economic face of society will alter, leading logically to a complete overhaul of the upper structures, including the political, constitutional and legal systems.

As technology and production processes continue to *change*, the forces of production themselves evolve and become more sophisticated with the passage of time. Hence, a socio-economic system (with its associated relationships) that was acceptable at a certain phase of society's development may become unacceptable at another phase, thus setting off conflicts and resulting in yet another socio-economic set-up. As this process continues, yesterday's friends of the production forces may become enemies, and the social make-up of society will *keep changing*.

The ever-present premise of Marxism is that at every turning point of society's evolution, the productive forces will attain *victory* at the expense of those whose interests lie with the then prevailing production/ownership relationships. In a parallel fashion, the social classes which support those forces at each battle will end up in an advantageous position, while those at the other side of the social divide will lose out.

Economic circumstances, along with their interlinked production/ownership relationships, will stay without change, as long as society continues to function within the confines of a given phase, while the productive forces preserve their features and develop within those confines. However, once the development of the productive forces became relatively dramatic, and current relations become a hindrance, conflict will ensue and change will follow, so that a new phase will be created. And so on, the process continues, producing new social classes and a new socio-economic set-up every time a major change takes effect.

1.3 PRACTICALITY OF HISTORICAL MATER-IALISM

Marxists have been maintaining that historical materialism is the *only* sound and practical way to comprehend history in an objective fashion. Some Marxists have even accused opponents of the theory of being *enemies* of the science of history, as well as oblivious to objective truths.

These Marxist contentions rest on *two* bases as follows:

A)   the belief that an objective truth does *exist* to explain the movement of history.

B)   that historical events do *not* come about through accident, and must therefore occur for a reason, which can be explored and ascertained.

However, does *any* opposition to the theory of historical materialism mean raising doubts over the existence of an objective truth? Is it not fallacious to insist that any scientific explanation of history *must* be within the framework of historical materialism.

The only alternative that Marxists admit to historical materialism is **idealism**, which asserts that the complete truth lies in our consciousness and feelings, but beyond the normal reach of our sensual environment.   Marxists regard such an explanation as unscientific and far removed from objective ascertainable analysis.

However, such *dualism* (i.e. idealism versus historical materialism) is unfair, and in fact fallacious. The clear aim of this standpoint is to level scorn at opponents of historical materialism, so as to accuse them of being dreaming idealists, not recognising the real world in which they live. And, it must be said that the focus on realism and a conviction in the objective analysis of history is not the *preserve* of Marxists. Nor can the rejection of historical materialism be viewed as *tantamount* to the denial of reality and truth.

All objective analysts of history agree that events occur because of *underlying* factors, and these may be related to race, natural phenomena or any other explanation. The **principle of causality** applies to historical developments as it relates to any other events, asserting that nothing happens without a given cause or plurality of causes that bring it about.

It is therefore possible to state that a belief in the objective analysis of history, along with a conviction in the principle of causality, are the two **hallmarks** of any scientific study of history. Debate can be complex and multi-faceted in this connection, as various factors may be put forward, and different social forces in society may be regarded as instrumental in accomplishing change.

Could these causes (or forces) be ideas or race? Or may be they are embodied in productive forces or natural phenomena. Alternatively, there may be a different cause (or a combination of causes) for each single event. Wherever the truth may lie, any investigation on those lines, if rationally and objectively conducted, can be seen as a scientific attempt to explain history.

~ *Chapter Two* ~

Philosophical Foundations of Marxism

An essential feature of Marxism is the emphasis on the **material aspect** in rationalising all phenomena, including historical events and developments. It is from this angel that Marxists ridicule 18th century materialism, regarding it as *idealistic* in outlook. The element of idealism is due primarily to the spiritual content in that analysis, according to Marxist thinking.

Marxists believe that idealism is *superficial*, not being sufficiently deep in analysing the true movers of events and developments. In the words of Engles

2.1   ON PHILOSOPHICAL MATERIALISM

It is important here to distinguish between *philosophical* materialism and *historical* materialism. The first can be described as:

Materialism *is the only truth in the universe. It encompasses all phenomena, and relates to every existence or being. Even matters spiritual, with related concepts, feelings, and abstractions, are manifestations of material output in special ways or particular fashions.*

No matter how complex or sophisticated is thinking, it remains an activity of the **brain**, which has a material existence. This means that all ideas emanating from humans - including any spiritual ingredients - can be encapsulated within the materialistic framework, when this is taken in its fullest and widest interpretation.

It also follows from this description of philosophical materialism, that **humans** could be a *product of materials* and the productive forces. It is equally possible for humans to have produced the conditions for production, including the various means required for that. An explanation of history can, therefore, start from either point, i.e. the existence of man/woman, or the availability of productive forces.

It is clear from this that the materialistic approach in philosophy does not necessarily accord with the Marxist view of history. The latter brings man/woman to a *lower* level in the historical ladder, as people are regarded as easily-moulded materials, who can be adjusted by the means of production.

2.2   NATURE OF DIALECTICS

Dialectics attempts to explain all events and developments as resulting form *conflicts*. What is more, this concept assumes that the seeds of conflict are present in every development or phenomenon, and that this ingredient grows more pronounced until such time when conflict comes out clearly to the open, and a decisive change or revolution occurs.

In effect, this is based on the old **Hegelian concept** of thesis , and-thesis and synthesis[1]. Every state of affairs (*thesis*) contains within it an element of opposition or contradiction (*anti-thesis*). As time goes by, the anti-thesis becomes stronger and more sophisticated,

---

[1] See H Landreth & D C Colander:
'History of Economic Thought' Houghton Mifflin Company, 1994, Page 176.

until it becomes capable of challenging the *status quo*. As a result of the ensuing conflict, a new situation evolves that tends to be a compromise (*synthesis*) of the two previously opposing forces. Once this settles, it in turn becomes a thesis bearing its own seeds of conflict, and thus the process continues.

Marxism *applies* dialectics to the social arena, utilising the dialectic methodology in analysing historical events. It envisages **class conflict** at the heart of any society, predicting that social growth and development will be a dynamic process resulting from internal struggles.

Marxist ideology believes that society's development is *not* pushed through by external or mechanical factors, but via its *own* ingredients which create conflicts; in time these conflicts produce change. Marxism affirms that class struggles will accumulate gradually, until an opportune time arrives when a complete transformation becomes possible, whereby the whole structure of society will be radically altered. Dialectic thinking recognises the importance of small and piecemeal quantitative changes, which build up towards major qualitative transformations.

2.2.1 Dialectic Method

It is important to note that Marxism has *utilised* the dialectic methodology *not* merely in historical analysis, but also in *other* areas of analytic study. However, Marxist thought has been caught by the **clash** of the dialectic method with the principle of causality.

For one thing, Marxist thought focuses on the role of **internal** conflicts in bringing about change. Yet, at the same time, Marxists concede the principle of causality, and *admit* the possible significance of external factors. This is a clear **contradiction** in Marxist analysis, which is glaringly obvious in studying historical developments.

The Marxist claim that changes in upper structures (e.g. legal and political systems) are caused by changes in the forces of production indicates the existence of a **causality** relationship between these two. This in turn means that changes in upper structures have *not* been brought about through internal conflicts in the dialectic mould, but via factors external to their core make-up.

Moreover, an argument can be made out to show that Marxist-envisaged change happens because of a contradiction between two *separate* things, namely old property relationships and newly developed forces of production. Could it not be said that we have in reality a clash between two separate things, *instead* of a contradiction within one thing?

Marxists seem to have realised this **predicament**, sandwiched as their argument is *between* the law of causality and the notion of dialectics. To attain an accommodation, Marxists have given the former a *special* dialectic meaning. They have therefore refuted the simple and straightforward connotation of the causality principle, where the cause remains an outside factor, while the effect assumes a passive stance.

In Marxist ideology, such a causality relationship contravenes the essential nature of dialectics, because the outcome can *not* be richer or more sophisticated than the cause. In contrast, Marxists are eager to make us believe that the end-product, which is the consequence of internal conflict, *is* better and more advanced than the thesis and anti-thesis.

In more precise terms, the **thesis** is viewed by Marxists as the *cause* that leads to a given phenomenon, while the **anti-thesis** is the *effect*. The **synthesis**, which as compromise that is ostensibly superior to both, is a compound, mixing elements of the thesis and anti-thesis. This notion of **dialectic causality** has been utilised by Marxists in their theorising of history, in order to support their contentions and particular line of thinking.

2.2.2 Falsification of Historical Dialectics

It must be made clear at this point that the notion of **dialectic causality** is not soundly-based, nor does it stand to rigors of philosophical analysis. There are **no** situations in science where such a causality has been proven, while philosophical research refutes it totally.

In order to show the **failure** of this line of thinking (i.e. dialectic causality) in the field of history, a pertinent case can be looked at. In Karl Marx's writings on the development of society to the capitalist stage, then to socialism, he refers to private ownership of the means of production in the following terms:

"The capitalist mode of appropriation, the result of the capitalist mode of production, produces capitalist private property. This is the first negation of individual private property, as founded on the labour of the proprietor. But capitalist production begets with the inexorability of a law of Nature its own negation. It is the negation of negation. This does not re-establish private property of the producer, but gives him individual property based on the acquisition of the capitalist era, i.e. on co-operation and the possession in common of the land and of the means of production".[2]

The **gist** of all this is that the result develops, so as to merge with the cause, to produce a compound that is **more sophisticated** than both. The property of the craftsman is the **thesis** (cause). When a capitalist takes over this small business, we have an **anti-thesis** (product). As this latter grows and becomes more sophisticated, it combines with the cause to form a new **compromise**, which is 'socialism', where the trader returns again as the owner of the means of production in a fashion that is more perfect.

However, history **cannot** be rationalised in such a fashion. This is an abstract argument, which Marx developed in **cognitive** style, rather

---

[2] C J Arthur: "Marx's Capital" Lawrence & Wishart, London, 1992, Page 378.

than real dialectics. How could the tiny property of a craftsman be the cause for a capitalist to take it over, so that it can be said that the anti-thesis (capitalism) resulted from the thesis (small-scale craft-based production)?

It is erroneous to suppose that capitalist production **resulted** form craftsmanship. Capitalism has come about as a consequence of the transformation of traders to medium-sized, and then large industrialists, as a result of certain conditions being fulfilled, including accumulation of wealth and availability of worthwhile opportunities. In fact, there is some evidence for the contention that capitalists regarded craftsmen as a hindrance to their ambitions and business strategies, and therefore utilised various methods to eradicate them, so as to expand capitalist production.

The **replacement** of individual craft-based output by the capitalist system is **not** similar to the birth of an anti-thesis from thesis. Capitalist production developed because a conducive business environment became a reality, leading in the process to the displacement/take-over of craft-based production. In effect, this boils down to the following conclusion:

Capitalist production *was caused via important external factors, such as the exploitation of mines, the opening up of overseas markets, and lucrative benefits of colonialism. Such factors bestowed upon the merchant class great financial advantages, thus enabling them to set-up capitalist production.*

2.2.3 Result Contravenes Method

What was spelled out above was a **catastrophic** result for Marxism. The method that it utilised (i.e. dialectic causality) brought it eventually to a point well removed form dialectics. So, while the Marxist methodology in analysing history is **dialectic**, the true essence of the cause-effect relationship is **not** dialectic.

For Marxism, the class struggle is the **touchstone** upon which the whole movement of history depends, resulting eventually in the **classless** society that Marxists seek.   But when socialism and communism are accomplished, the pattern of development will be *stalled*, thus spawning a miracle that will paralyse the dialectic process, as class conflict is no longer there.

If however the dialectic process of history will continue, then *what* is the anti-thesis of socialism? And what *will* be the synthesis? Because communism is viewed by Marxists as the most sophisticated phase of human society, will *all* class conflict cease at that stage? If it does, then is that *not* the end of progress? If conflict goes on, then what *will* be the outcome?

2.3   ON HISTORICAL MATERIALISM

it is the *central contention* of historical materialism that the economic situation of any society is the realistic basis for understanding that society in all its differing yet related aspects. All types of concepts and knowledge are explained, appraised and comprehended in this light. Consequently, human knowledge is not merely the fruits of the functional activity of the brain, but is **connected** also to economic circumstances. The human mind is a reflection of economic conditions and social relationships, in which people find themselves.

The Marxist **theory of knowledge** is based on this, which means that knowledge is relative and developing with time.   Therefore, knowledge has a relative value, which is constrained by prevailing conditions, though developing as circumstances alter. The upshot of this is that there is *no* absolute truth, but truths become uncovered gradually, as social relations allow and as society develops.

However, Marxism does *not* apply this very concept to the theory of historical materialism. If all knowledge was *relative*, then this theory must be susceptible to development and improvement - just like any other! In other words, the theory of historical materialism must have sprung up through a given socio-economic set-up, and hence liable to be changed and amended.

In this context, Marx regarded **revolution** as a necessary condition for accomplishing major changes. Also, revolution would come about as a result of a clash between two large social classes, such as the *bourgeoisie* and the *proletariat*. This line of thinking matured sufficiently in Marx's mind, when he noticed the detailed complexities of 19th century social and economic environment, which was characterised by sharply rising *gaps* in wealth, health and knowledge, concluding - as he did - that revolution was *inevitable*.

But as we now know, the conditions of misery and deprivation that dogged the working classes were gradually *alleviated*. Hence social conflict did not intensify, but in fact receded and became more restrained, especially after the death of Karl Marx. Case after case came to prove that it was *not* necessary for revolution to take place, and that it was perfectly possible for the general public to gain important concessions, through the normal political process.

This *split* the Marxist movement into two main *strands*, one radical and revolutionary, the other democratic and reformist. The latter became the dominant socialist current in Western Europe, while the former gained the upper hand in the former Soviet Union and Eastern Europe[3].

This **dichotomy** led to sharp differences between the two sides. While the socialist movement in Western Europe saw in the *ballot box* a path for politico-economic advancement on the requisite road, their counterparts in the East regarded *revolution* as the true embodiment of Marxism, both in its seedlings and eventual fulfilment.

---

[3] It can be said that democratic - inclined socialism became popular in these latter countries by the late 1980's, when the old regimes disintegrated one after the other.

All this indicates the constrained nature of Marxist ideology, in the sense that it really reflected Marx's understandings based on the particular conditions that existed at the time. As a result, Marxist revolution can not be viewed as a historical fact, as supported amply by the practical experience of Western Europe.

In conclusion, two **main points** can be spelled out:

<u>First</u>: some theories and concepts are influenced by the *objective conditions* of society, so much so that those theories/concepts may appear - rather mistakenly - to reflect concrete truths, while in fact they are valid only in the context of the relevant conditions. Some of Marx's notions of history fall within this category.

<u>Second</u>: all Marxist notions on history must be viewed as *relative*. They rest on the validity of socio-economic relationships that were current at the time when Marxism was developed, and therefore they need to develop with those relationships. Hence, historical materialism is not a fact of history, because all theories are products of the stage when they are evolved, as Marxists themselves insist.

~ *Chapter Three* ~

General Framework of Marxist Thought

It is now necessary to study the **general theory** of Marxism, without looking at the fine details. Several questions need to be put forward in this regard, *major* among which are the following three:

<u>First</u>: what evidence is there to prove that the state of productive forces *determines* the movement of history?

<u>Second</u>: is there some type of measure to *weigh up* scientific theories? If so, how does Marxism *fare up* in this connection?

<u>Third</u>: has the theory of historical materialism been able to *plug* all the holes in human history? Or are there some aspects of human life that are still *outside* the bounds of the materialistic explanation of history?

3.1 EVIDENCE FOR HISTORICAL MATERIALISM

In the main, the **evidence** on which historical materialism is based may be divided into three categories:
* philosophical evidence
* psychological evidence
* scientific evidence

3.1.1 Philosophical Evidence

This is simply evidence based on **philosophical analysis** of the problem, as distinct from experiment and observation throughout the different phases of history.   In essence, the philosophical evidence for historical materialism can be summed up thus:

historical events follow the principle of causality, which forces us to search for the factors behind any development.

It is clear, for example, that modern European society is *different* from what it was ten centuries ago. A reason must, therefore, exist for this difference. We need to find an explanation for **every** change or development in the social set-up, in a way that is analogous to the methods used by a natural scientist, e.g. in physics or chemistry, to identify the cause for every effect.

It *may* be said that all changes in history are due to changes in ideology or viewpoint.   But *is* this explanation **sufficient**?   Do people's viewpoints alter by chance, or are they brought about by certain factors?

Why, for instance, has the concept of **political liberty** (for individuals, parties etc.) become so fundamental today, in contrast to prevailing European thinking in the Middle Ages? Again, why has there been criticisms of the concept of **private property** during our times, as compared with the past?

We may resort to the social make-up as the main factor, or we may view a given aspect of society (e.g. economic circumstances) as being responsible. But such a rationalisation solves none of our problems, because questions can be raised concerning the factor(s) behind any **alterations** in a society's make-up or its detailed circumstances. To square this circle, we may adopt one of the following *two* approaches:

A) we can go back one step, so as to repeat our previous assertion that ideology and viewpoint are the **source** of change in society. But this results in a vicious circle, as the social make-up has already been singled out as the factor behind developments in ideology and viewpoint. In fact, this is the path taken by historians who have relied on **realism** to explain historical developments.

B) we can adopt Marxist thinking in attempting to find a cause-effect relationship. This leads us to the **forces of production** as the main factor behind change, and an ultimate cause for changes in society and movement in history.

In analysing this latter view, it is necessary to recognise first that the forces of production do *not* remain still. They change and develop with time, and as human ideology and social conditions alter. But *why* do productive forces change and develop?

The Marxist answer to this crucial matter is that as humans utilise the means of production, **new ideas** arise and develop. Such ideas, and consequent scientific knowledge, are a product of experimentation, flowing from using natural productive forces. The obvious result of all this is the *adaptation* of current productive forces and development of new ones. Thus Marxism has given prime place to the forces of production, *without* admitting clearly and fully the role of **contemplation** and **creative thinking**.

Friedrich Engels had actually recognised this kind of explanation, indicating that the concept of dialectics did *not* regard cause and effect as two sharply opposing poles, as some non-dialectics had chosen to understand them. Those who believed in dialectics, according to Engels, viewed the cause-effect relationships a sort of *action and reaction* of forces.

This is all very well. But why cannot we apply this reasoning to the social circumstances, in which people are involved? As the forces of production are developed *through* creative thinking, so can the social setting become more mature and sophisticated via the accumulated experience of ordinary individuals, who bring to bear their own contemplation for the welfare of society as whole, or any specific part of it.

The next issue that can be raised is this: why is it *always* necessary to involve the forces (or means) of production in explaining history? Is it not possible - in some cases at least - that social change can be effected through **creative thinking-cum-contemplation**, and in turn social change can cause *additional* developments in thinking? At least the writings of Engels seem to allow this.

3.1.2 Psychological Evidence

The starting point here is the attempt to show that thought *began* as a product of certain social phenomena. It follows from this that social structures *preceded* human thought. Marxists would have us believe that, as a result of this, for any society to be analysed scientifically, this has to be done *within* the context of materialism.

This is amply put by Joseph V Stalin, when he writes that 'thought is a product of matter, which in its development has reached a high degree of perfection, namely of the brain, and the brain is the organ of thought. Therefore, one cannot separate thought from matter.'[1] Maurice Cornforth amplify this by adding :

' A man is endowed with a mind, then in so far as he thinks, feels, desires, and so on. But all these activities are activities, functions, of the man, of a material being, an organised body, dependent on appropriate bodily organs. Given a body with the appropriate organisation and appropriate conditions of life, these activities arise and develop. Destroy the body or its organs, and these activities are destroyed with it. All the mental functions and activities, which are

---

[1] J V Stalin : 'Dialectical and Historical Materialism' cited in Maurice Cornforth : 'Dialectical Materialism : Theory of Knowledge' Volume 3,   published by Lawrence & Wishart, London,1956, Page 14

said to be products of mind, as distinct from matter, are products of matter. The mind is a product of matter.'[2]

But *how* does Marxism look at the link between ideas and language? The Marxist view is that ideas are the result of **language**, and the latter is nothing more than a social phenomenon. Also, no ideology can be conceived without language, and therefore all thinking is an *ancillary* aspect of social living.

All this raises the following *major* issues: is it true that language is the *basis* of thinking? And is language what made human *thinking creatures*? or alternatively, is it more accurate to say that language found its place, in the life of the thinking man/woman, due to the presence of *ideas* that wanted an outlet of expression?

It is pertinent here to refer to the *ideas* put forward by Pavlov, regarding the interpretation of thinking in a *physiological* manner. Pavlov proved that when a **link** is made between a natural stimulant and something else, then the latter will *acquire* the associated activity or property of the stimulant, performing its function and producing the same response. So, when a bell is associated in a dog's mind with feeding time, then the bell will produce the craving even where there is *no* food being served. The bell became known as *conditional stimulant*, while the craving *conditional response*.

Some have attempted to explain *all* human thought on the basis of physiological rationalisation, on lines similar to the above illustration. In this context, all human thinking is *in response* to stimulants. For members of the human race, there are natural stimulants, resulting in commensurate responses, which we have become accustomed to regard as types of **comprehension**. All **tools** of communication are thus viewed as 'conditional stimulants'. For example, the word 'water' releases the same effect as actually *feeling* that basic substance.

---

[2] Ibid.

In Pavlov's view, individuals cannot think without stimulants, because the process of thinking is nothing more than a **reaction** to stimulants. Abstract contemplation would **not** be possible without conditional stimulants that are associated with feelings, and the former would release **similar responses** to those caused by the associated feelings.

Even if we **concede** all this, do we have to agree that language is the basis of **all** human thinking? The answer is **No**! In certain instances, it does happen that something is **associated** with a realistic (natural) event (stimulant), e.g. a sound indicating the flow of water. While **many** examples of this type of association have accumulated throughout human history, it would be **wrong** to assert that this is the only conduit for language development, and consequently any sort of thinking.

The tools of language have evolved due to the **needs** of social interaction. Individuals constantly require to express their ideas, and convey them to others. This means that language fulfils a **central role** in human existence, because individuals are by their nature thinking creatures, who need to communicate their thoughts.

It is therefore **erroneous** to insist that language is the basis of all thinking. Rather, it is *a channel for communicating human thought*, and has been so since early times. Language is a fundamental social phenomenon, which has resulted from the need for expressing all sorts of ideas, instead of being the basis for producing a thinking creature.

On this basis, we can understand why language performs such a pervasive and wide-ranging function in human life, in contrast in other living creatures. Men and women can **transcend** the boundaries of their material senses, so as to alter the objective environment in which they live. Other living creatures possess **no** comparable ability to contemplate, and therefore their thinking is limited by their material senses, a fact that does not enable them to change their environment.

The ability of accomplishing change in the objective environment is **special** to mankind, and requires a variety of efforts which often assumes a social dimension. When people get involved in joint activities to change the environment, they need a language as a communication medium, so as to describe and quantify links among various things requiring adjustment or change.

3.1.3 Scientific Evidence

The scientific explanation of phenomena adopts a *step-by-step* approach. At first, a hypothesis is made, then a proof is sought to ascertain that hypothesis. If the proof was forthcoming, the hypothesis is accepted, otherwise it is refuted. In similar vein, historical materialism is a **hypothesis** that requires proof beyond all reasonable doubt.

Let's look, then, at the rationalisation given by historical materialism for the existence of the **State**. This is based on the economic factor and the related concept of class struggle. Struggle is the hallmark of conflict-ridden society, whereby the stronger property-owning class will prevail over weaker classes that are dispossessed. The former will take the initiative to set-up a political **entity** to protect their economic interests, in the form of a government, whatever that form might have taken throughout history.

This explanation *cannot* stand the test, unless it can be proved that the State *is* set-up and utilised as a tool for class exploitation. If, however, we can prove that some *other* explanation exist for the existence of the State, then the Marxist hypothesis in this regard must be rejected.

When it can be shown, for instance, that the birth of State institutions was due to the complexity of civil life, then the theory of historical materialism is refuted. This, in fact, was the case in ancient

Egypt, where the ruling class were mainly experts in the fields of agriculture and irrigation, rather than by virtue of belonging to a dominant social class.

A further example can be quoted from the Roman Empire, where the clergy enjoyed immense State authority during a certain epoch. This was primarily due to the relative intellectual advantage of top Church officials at that time, a fact which enabled them - among other things - to be literate, speak Latin and count months, days etc. They were thus ideal bureaucrats, thereby possessing power to manage government organs and being highly influential in the political arena. While their privileged positions enabled them to gain subsequent economic advantage, it was not the latter which made them ascend to high political office.

It can, therefore, be said that any realistic evidence showing that **religious faith** was instrumental in establishing the State would directly contradict Marxist analysis. In addition to religious authority, there have been other bases put forward to explain the setting up of the State - quite apart from the Marxist doctrine of economic power.

It is pretty clear that Marxism faces a major **problem** in proving scientifically the correctness of the theory of historic materialism. This is due to the social nature of historical studies, as distinct from the exactness characterising pure science, such as physics and chemistry. In the case of the latter, scientists study and analyse natural phenomena (e.g. light, heat, sound) under controlled laboratory conditions. In contrast, historians have to explain past events in human society (e.g. social evolution and development), and would therefore need to *rely* on verbal accounts or descriptions by others. In most cases, it is possible for researchers in fields of pure-science to observe the phenomena directly, while it is rare for historical analysts to have that type of opportunity.

In pure-science research, it is generally possible to utilise **experimentation**, in order to make logical inferences. Even where such experimentation is not possible (e.g. in astronomy), scientists may be able to vary their relationship/angle vis-à-vis the object being studied, via repositioning the telescope or changing the observation point etc. Such possibilities for change/experimentation are ***denied*** to the history analyst/scientist.

For instance, it is ***not*** possible for historical researchers to use certain **experimental techniques**, that accord with experimental logic, in their attempts to uncover the main factor(s) behind a given historical phenomenon. Exact-science researchers can use the main two methods in experimental inference, namely the methods of 'association' and 'difference', whereas these two are mostly ***impractical*** in the case of historical research. This is due to the impracticality of adding/eliminating various variables.

In effect, what remains for historical researches is synchronised and/or well-directed **observation**, in order to assimilate the largest amount possible of historical events. The main purpose is to explain those events as objectively and scientifically as possible. On this basis, Marxism did ***not*** really possess any scientific support for its particular notion of history, except some observation that Marxists considered sufficient.

The crux of all this is that in Engels's view the observation of social conditions over a given period in Europe (and England in particular) was **enough** to draw a firm scientific conclusion that the economic factor (along with class struggle) was the **prime determinant** in all human history. This is despite other historical evidence showing more murky situations.

3.2 SEARCH FOR A HIGHER CRITERION

It is a firm Marxist belief that in testing any theory, the litmus criterion is **applicability**. Marxists affirm that any theory must ***not*** be separated from reality, and this has given rise to the notion of ***unity of theory and practice***, in the realm of dialectics.

On that basis, it would be relevant to study the theory of historical materialism, with a view of assessing its chance of corroboration in practice. It is fit to note at the outset that a *rare* opportunity has been afforded to Marxism, in that a transformation from capitalism to socialism had taken place during this century. Yet, other aspects of Marxism, particularly those pertaining to previous historical epochs, have not been similarly corroborated or tested.

In any case, it is possible to divide countries where a transfer to socialism had been attempted into **two** main categories:

First: countries where the socialist system was *imposed* by the Red Army. These are mainly the countries of Eastern Europe and the Baltic States, where a socialist transformation did not occur in accord with Marxist ideology. This is quite separate from the acute practical problems that those nations experienced under the so-called socialist regimes, and the final collapse of those structures in the late 1980's.

Second: nations where socialism was instituted through *internal revolution*. These revolutions, however, did not embody Marxist laws. The experience of these nations did not correspond with Marxism theory, which attempted to solve the mysteries of history.

Russia was the first country where a socialist revolution succeeded, but in fact the country was relatively *undeveloped* compared to Western Europe, in terms of industrial progress and the sophistication of productive forces. Marxist theory stipulates that socialist revolution would be appropriate when productive forces reach their highest state of maturity and sophistication under capitalism.

In fact, what we witnessed during the 20th century was quite the *opposite* to the scenario that Marxism predicted. In countries such as Britain, France and Germany, much advancement and sophistication had been attained by the productive forces. But as industrialisation gathered pace, those nations became poles apart from following the path of communist outburst. By contrast,

Russian industrialisation was low-key, while local industrialists were unable to deal with the intricacies of rapid industrial advance, due to prevailing political and social conditions.

In effect, it can be said that political revolution in Russia *brought about* the requisite industrial revolution, rather than *vice versa*. The new ruling class in Moscow were highly instrumental in creating wide-ranging industrialisation of society, as well as developing the forces of production. Therefore, it is perfectly legitimate to say that in the case of that country, the low state of industrialisation was a major factor in *fermenting* revolution – quite the reverse of what Marxism stipulated.

Taking this a step further, it could be asserted that when Russians noticed their relative industrial backwardness, they chose to *radically* change the ruling elite, in order to join the developed world and avoid being left trailing behind. Otherwise, the country would have remained relatively underdeveloped and wide open to exploitation by major Western corporations – a scenario that would have ended Russia's sovereign economic status in the world.

It is therefore quite proper to *ask* the following question: *would there have been a socialist revolution in Russia, if that country was at a similar stage of economic, social, industrial and political advance as Western Europe?* Indeed, the dramatic collapse of the socialist system in the early 1990's meant that it gave way to capitalism, rather the other way round – indicating thus that the latter was *more* advanced than the former!

In case of China again shows that practice did *not* tally with Marxist thinking. Once more, an industrial revolution was not the fundamental factor in dispensing with the old regime and creating the New China. *No* part was played by the production forces, or the contradictions of capitalism, in the political arena.

It is also fair to say that where victory of socialist Marxism was accomplished, this was not a direct and clear consequence of class struggle and the disintegration of the ruling elite *vis-à-vis* the power of the masses. In practically all cases, the collapse of the *status quo* was military in nature, resulting from harsh war conditions, as was true in both Russia and China. In each of these two situations, an *outside* conflict played a crucial part.

In the case of Russia, there was the significant impact of World War I, while in China's case, there were the effects of the Japanese invasion. There is no doubt, however, that the strong communist leadership, coupled with effective party organisation, was instrumental in achieving victory. It is, therefore, clear that class struggle was *definitely* not alone in brining about change, as other factors also had their glaring influence.

To be sure, the two global wars during the 20th century did lead to internal strife and revolutions in a number of countries. In many of these situations, weak ineffectual State apparatuses were an important underlying factor; so did a widespread feeling of the need for rapid progress. However, the two cases which glaringly stand out as victories for socialism were Russia and China.

When comparing Russia and China, on the one hand, with other successful revolutions, on the other hand, it is not differences in productive forces that stand out, as these were not substantially different between the two sides. What does stand out, however, is the difference in ideology and the differing political currents between these two situations.

The firm conclusion, therefore, is that the theory of historical materialism still lacks empirical support. The victories that Marxism accomplished in practice did *not* bear out the supposed characteristics of the doctrine. In fact, there are grounds for asserting that the leaders of the Bolshevik revolution in Russia did *not* expect that speedy victory, and were indeed surprised by the outcome.

3.3   MARXISM AND ASSIMILATION OF HISTORY

There is no doubt that Marxism represents a wholly **integrated and analytic** system, that surpasses most other corresponding ideologies, in terms of covering the various socio-economic aspects and the interrelationships among them. The doctrine is not limited or narrow in its approach, nor is it merely a social or economic concept. Marxist ideology embodies a comprehensive analysis, relating to social, economic, and political ingredients, spanning thousands of years throughout human history, so as to assess results and consequence of every phenomenon or development.

It is, therefore, only to be expected that many people have shown their **respect** for this ideology, and expressed their admiration towards it. This is particularly so, as Marxists have assumed that they have uncovered the prime mysteries of human history and politico-economic change, in ways that are superior to any other scientific theory within the realms of economics, politics, and sociology. The doctrine has provided people with a scientific analysis of historical change, moderated by the general aspirations of the masses, in as much as Marx could foresee.

In Marxism, economic conditions are the cornerstone, linking the forces of production with all social phenomena. This comes clearly in the writings of Plekhanov.

The production forces, therefore, are the prime movers of the economic situation, and the latter will develop as a consequence of changes in the former. Furthermore, economic circumstances are the basis on which the whole social structure is built.

Writers who have **opposed** Marxism have put forward major arguments in this connection. Among these are the following two:

First: if history is indeed governed by the economic variable, then why should it be necessary for Marxists to exert such enormous efforts, in order to attain their objectives in defeating capitalism and setting up socialism?

They could allow the laws of history to work themselves, so as to save them all the trouble they are going through, in terms of mobilisation, organisation etc.

Second: every person feels - by necessity and instinct - that he/she is often motivated by factors other than pure money, and does at times sacrifice the latter for the sake of those other motivations.   In consequence, how can we assess the significance of the economic factor as a mover of history?

These two arguments do *not* diminish the importance of Marxism, as both covey *insufficient* understanding of Marxism. In the case of the first argument, Marxism views efforts to bring about revolution as an *integral* element of the laws of history.   Hence, when revolutionaries group themselves and plan their strategies and tactics, they are expressing an historical inevitability.

This is despite the fact that Marxists have not always understood clearly and fully the full requirements of their own theory on history.

This is a plain Marxist admission that people can have control over the laws of history, *via* their own thinking and other conscious activities.   But when history is driven by general and natural laws, then the actions or omissions of humans must be regarded as part of those laws, rather than superior to them. As an example, if Marxists attempt through various actions to speed up the demise of capitalism, so as to hasten the birth of the socialist State, they are acting *in accord* with the laws of history, as Marxist ideology requires.

We can now move to the second argument referred to above, which enquires about the place of non-economic influences on human behaviour.   Again, this anti-Marxist argument is a non-starter, because Marxists do *not* say that economic influences are necessarily the conscious motive for all human actions throughout history. They simply assert that economic factors are the power that expresses itself in people's consciousness in various ways. In effect, this implies that conscious and deliberate human behaviour is due to a variety of motives, but these are the *outward* cover for a real and deeper factor which pertains to economics.

In fact, some Marxist writings have even gone further than this, by suggesting that economic targets are the *ultimate* objectives for social activity, and not necessarily the moving force behind the scene. This line of reasoning indicates that power is a means to achieve the aim, which pertains to economic targets.

3.3.1 Development of Production Forces

Major questions can be addressed to Marxists concerning the development of productive forces. How does this occur? What factors determine this development? Why can we not regard these factors as the real movers of history, instead of the productive forces themselves?

According to Marxists, the factors that develop the productive forces emanate *from* these forces, rather than being independent from them. In essence, this development is due to the activity of the human brain, which benefits from experience and observation. All this results in what Marxists refers to as *dialectic development of production forces.*

It is pretty obvious here that the forces of production develop and mature because of a fundamental factor, namely the *human brain*, which stores, analyses and utilises a great deal of data relating to the external environment and the production setting, in addition to the process of thinking undertaken by the mind itself.

Marxism has not answered the question as to how production *first* began. If production can explain the beginning and development of society, what are then conditions for the *beginning* of production on our planet?

Marxism defines 'production' as a ***struggle against nature, in which people participate, in order to produce their material requirements, and on this basis certain human relationships develop***. It is therefore clear that production is an activity involving people, and it seeks to change nature and mould it in forms that correspond to human needs.

But all this could not have happened ***without*** the existence of two essential conditions:

First: ***thinking***, as this is bound to precede any conscious effort to manufacture, extract, render, plant, or re-shape any product or service.

Second: ***language***, as this is the material exterior of thought, so that participants in production activity may understand and co-operate with one another.

As a consequence, thought must ***precede*** the production process, while language emanates from the necessity for ***exchanging*** ideas. While language is by far the pivotal social phenomenon, it is not a result of the production process. If language was a by-product of production activities and the nature of the production set-up, then major language changes would have followed political revolutions (e.g. Bolshevik revolution in Russia) or technological breakthroughs (e.g. development of the steam engine in England).

3.3.2 Thought and Marxism

The link between economic conditions and human thought is perhaps the most ***critical*** element of the material explanation of history put forward by Marxist ideology.

From this, we can only deduce that Engels wanted to show that all thinkers were ignorant of the true factors behind their ideas, indicating - in the process - that only historical materialism could uncover those factors. More than this, does all this mean that Engels *alone* was able to single out the true motives and movers behind all ideology, producing what may be termed as a 'miracle'?

In this regard, it is pertinent to look at some major influences on ideology throughout human history:

First: Religion

There is little doubt that this factor has played a major part in formulating the human mind-set. As Marxism had shunned the realistic impact of religion, it had to find a materialistic explanation for this persistent and major ingredient of human culture.

A wide-spread view within materialistic circles was that religion resulted from the feebleness of the ancient man, his feelings of weakness *vis-à-vis* nature and its awesome powers, along with his ignorance of its mysteries and fundamental laws. But Marxism did *not* accept such a viewpoint, because it deviates from its central thesis, which regards production and production forces as the nucleus of all reasoning.

It is a firm Marxist belief that the birth and evolution of religion can be traced to the class make-up of society. In Marx's opinion, it is the miserable conditions experienced by the oppressed class which give rise to religious beliefs, in order to draw consolation and assurance.

In essence, Marxists have focused on saying that religion is the **consequence** of the class struggle in society, but different writers have given differing accounts of this. Some have maintained that religion is the opium administered by the ruling elite to the oppressed and helpless masses, so that these can forget about their demands and political significance in society. This would lead them to accept subjugation, acquiescing to the prevailing hapless state in which they find themselves. In effect, this means that religion is a web woven by the governing class to hunt the poor, and to lure and keep them under control.

But all this shows how oblivious Marxists have been of glaring historical facts, which tell us that religion **begins** inevitably among the poor and dispossessed, then it permeates all sections of society. This is very clear in Christianity, the banner of which was hoisted high by impoverished apostles, who had nothing but he spiritual torch within their souls, and were able to spread the message throughout the globe. Islam began in similar vein, whereby the core of early advocates were - for the most part - either poor or semi-poor.

If now we look briefly at the rise of these two great religions - Christianity and Islam - we find some major elements that could **not** have been pleasing to those holding economic and political power at the time. How could the prohibition of usury be a blessing to usury-practising capitalists who were gleaning enormous profits form such a system? Or how could the call for equality among people and the insistence on human dignity (even to the extent of occasionally denigrating the rich and condemning their arrogance) be music to the ears of those holding the reigns of politico-economic power?

In other cases, Marxists have claimed that religion **emanates** from the deepness of frustration and destitution. The oppressed masses find faith and assurance in religion, so as to breathe a ray of hope in their life. Religion is, therefore, the ideology of the have-nots and frustrated, and **not** a ploy created by rulers.

Fortunately, religion is **not** an ideological phenomenon associated only with class-demarcated societies. Evidence suggests that religion was present even in communities viewed by Marxists to have lived and practised a communist classless existence. This means that **no** meaning to religion can be given within the exclusive context of societies characterised by class-related differences and struggles. Nor does such evidence permit us to regard religion as a cognitive reflection towards the oppression engulfing the hard-pressed struggling classes, as that evidence corroborates the contention that religious beliefs existed in class-free communities.

In addition, how is it possible for Marxists to explain the religious beliefs of those who are *not* on the receiving end of exploitation? How could the well-off and reasonably-endowed embrace beliefs and ideologies evolved and elaborated essentially by those much less fortunate than them? It is not possible for Marxists to deny the strength of religious beliefs held by some people who have not been subjected to exploitation or oppression, to the degree that these people might be ready to sacrifice their wealth, or even their lives, for the sake of those beliefs.

All this proves that religion does not always result from economic circumstances. In many cases, religious ideas have been a reflection of people's psychic and mental processes - as distinct form economic conditions - leading them to ideological beliefs.

It has to be said that the Marxist class-content explanation of religion does not stop here. It goes further by assuming that religion *develops* with changes in economic circumstances. As a nation's economic conditions advance - we are told - the gods worshipped by a nation possess a national dimension, not transcending the boundaries of that country. When national divides are superseded, and empires were established (e.g. Roman Empire, Ottoman Empire), new trans-national gods became necessary.
However, when we look at historical facts, we find that things do *not* quite tally with this. It took some 250 years for Christianity to become the established religion of the Roman Empire, and during that epoch religion was adapted to feudal conditions. Then, when the Catholic version of Christianity clashed with the interests of the growing bourgeois, reform movements began to appear.

If Christianity was a response to materialistic and objective requirements - as Marxism would have it - then it would have been more natural for Christianity to be born at the *heart* of the Roman Empire, while the Reformation ought to have started in the

European countries which were most developed. Instead, the prime seeds of Christianity were concentrated in one of the Eastern regions colonised by the Romans, and grew among an oppressed Jewish nation, whose chief aspiration was to gain national independence and destroy all links with the imperialists.

As for religious reform movements, these were spawned mainly by the currents of *liberal* ideology within Europe, and were **not** the consequence of the growth of bourgeois powers. While this latter class did actually benefit from the so-called **Reformation**, it would be wrong to assert that the latter grew out merely from the expansion of bourgeois economic power.

In addition, as **England** was the country characterised by the highest level of bourgeois development in Europe, Reformation ought to have started in that country. Instead, the main seeds of Protestantism appeared in Germany and France, despite the fact that England had by then attained an impressive and relatively advanced degree of politico-economic progress.

If now we look at Islam and the Marxist view regarding religious development, we find an obvious **contradiction** between ideology and practice. In Europe, there was a global State (Roman Empire) requiring a global religion. But in the Arabian peninsula there was **not** even a national State, let alone a global one! In fact, the Arabs were, at that time, split among various tribes, each with a god made of stone, to which members prostrate and owe allegiance! Were these the materialistic and political conditions providing for the birth of a new globalised religion at the heart of the desert?

Second: Philosophy

It is a firm Marxist belief that **'philosophy'** is another cognitive phenomenon of life's materialism and associated economic conditions experienced by society, and an inevitable result of that life.

There is no denying that a relationship exists between **ideology**, on the one hand, and materialistic and economic **conditions** experienced by thinkers, on the other. Likewise, it is not possible to refute that ideology has its special nature and relevant principles, because thought must be subject to the same influences that are universally present in this world, in accord with the law of causality. Each ideological development/phenomenon has its *own* reasons, that bring it about. However, according to Marxism, the real underlying factor for ideological phenomena can be found in economic and materialistic conditions.

Many extracts can be quoted from Marxist writings to show this **emphasis** on the economic factor as an explanation of ideology. According to Marxism, there is *no* independent or separate history of ideology, as it is merely a repercussion for the cognitive reflections provoked by the economic and materialistic conditions of society.

This is quite clear in the writings of communist thinkers, such as Maurice Cornforth, who maintains that as the tools of production are developed and renewed, *new* concepts are born in the *minds* of philosophers. Such progress - we are told by Marxist writers - has put to rest the rigid viewpoint towards the Universe, bringing about a revolutionary outlook, in a parallel fashion with changes in the means of production.

Quoting F Engels, Cornforth adds that 'the production of the immediate material means of subsistence, and consequently the degree of economic development attained by a given people or during a given epoch, form the foundation upon which the State institutions, the legal conceptions, the ideas on art, and even on religion, of the people concerned have been evolved'[3]

However, if we look at the major revolutions in the methods of production, we find this mainly started in the second half of the 18th century, with the advent of steam power. But we find, in fact, that a

---

[3] M Cornforth : 'Dialectical Materialism : Historical Materialism' Volume 2, published by Lawrence & Wishart, London,1953, Page 49

cardinal contribution to materialistic philosophy was made by Diderot, who wrote in the first half of the 18th century, stressing that material develops *by itself*, and expounding the whole philosophy of life on this basis. While there is no denying that radical changes in the field of production have often prepared the mind-set for accepting philosophical advances, there is *no* sufficient evidence to indicate an ever-lasting causality relationship.

In fact, it can be said quite categorically that no *logically* permanent link can be asserted between the system of production, on the one hand, and developments in philosophy, on the other. **Three** cases in point can be mentioned here:

The first is the Greek philosopher **Anaximander**, who lived during the 6th century BC, and who developed a philosophical notion on evolution, asserting that living organisms start at a low-state and advance gradually due to innate factors, which provide for adjustment with the surrounding environment. Humans - according to this theory - were living in water, and got adapted to dry land as water receded.

The second is **Heraclitus**, whom Marxists regard as an excellent exponent of the essence of dialectics and the associated concept of evolution. Heraclitus lived during the 5th century BC and developed his notion of dialectics-based evolution, emphasising that the universe with all its contents are in a state of flux. This expresses contradictions, as all moving objects have an existence though they keep changing. All this was long before natural science had been born, and certainly before any astronomical discoveries.

The third case is that of the Muslim scholar **Sadruldeen AL-Shirazi**, who brought about nothing less than a revolution in Islamic philosophy in the early 17th century. He proved that the universe, by its very nature, keeps changing, showing through abstract philosophical reasoning that continuous development is at the core of all our being and environment. All this was at a time when practically everything in social life was virtually static.

In addition, historical evidence does **not** support the link between philosophical ideas, on the one hand, and economic circumstances and the state of production forces, on the other. In Europe, the first harbingers of the new ideological revolution appeared not in England (which was more economically developed) but in France during the 13th and 14th centuries.

While the English nation was at the forefront in terms of economic advancement, and accomplished significant political progress beginning from the 13th century, this was not fully reflected in terms of philosophical progress attained. Two 14th century French thinkers (Pierre Orival and Duran de San Boursan) can be viewed as the pioneers in the field of materialistic philosophy. While Karl Marx claimed that materialism was first developed by the English thinker Francis Bacon, we find in fact that Bacon was very much an idealist and called for experimentation in research.

As for the relationship between philosophy and natural science, it is difficult to link all philosophical development to advances in pure science. Because it is quite possible for philosophical thinking to precede scientific achievements, it would be wrong to make the former depend on the latter.

The final point that needs to be dealt with in this regard concerns the link between class and philosophy, as Marxism emphasises such a relationship. In the words of Maurice Cornforth 'ideas are always formed according to the needs of social intercourse. And with the development of production and consequent development of production relations, and of social relations and social activity generally, ideas are developed beyond the limited stage of consciousness of the common features of objects perceived through the senses. Men form general concepts and views about the world and their own social life. Such more abstract ideas are formed in men's minds as a product of their active relationship to external nature and to one another, and serve the development of social intercourse based on those relationships..'[4]

Even such generalised statements are unacceptable to Marxists, who maintain that **'idealistic philosophy'** - a term that Marxists use to refer to all philosophical theses which shun the materialist approach - is that of the ruling elite and the exploitive minority, in order to stay in power. The antidote of that is **materialistic philosophy**, which is the one held by the oppressed masses.

Third: Science

It is a firm Marxist belief that the natural sciences grow and develop in response to materialistic requirements, which have to be understood within the context of economic circumstances. As these circumstances are primarily the historic consequence of the production forces and productive techniques, then ultimately the latter are the real determinants of scientific advance.

Each epoch of history becomes adjusted to economic circumstances, and contributes towards scientific progress, in as much as the economic situation requires. So, when steam power was discovered during the late 18th century, this was the pure consequence of economic conditions and capitalists' need for great power to propel their machines. Other discoveries and scientific developments are viewed in similar light.

Four main comments can be made regarding this supposed link between science and the state of productive forces, as follows:

i) if we put aside the gigantic scientific developments of modern times, we note that previous generations had gone along with essentially *similar* working methods. This is particularly clear and well documented with regard to the two main primary sectors in any society, namely agriculture and industry.

---

[4] Maurice Cornforth : 'Dialectical Materialism : Theory of Knowledge' Volume 3, Op. Cit., Pages 71-2

Despite this, however, the level of scientific advance in those multi-various societies differed greatly. Such discrepancies in terms of knowledge and scientific attainments were very glaring between, say, Europe of the Middle Ages and Muslim communities at those times (e.g. Iraq, Egypt, and Andalucia), while the production base was essentially the same.

Also, how could the ancient Chinese invent printing, while other communities could not acquire that technology, except via China? Muslims were able to obtain printing technology form the Chinese in the 8th century DC, and it was transferred to Europe through the Muslims in the 13th century. In this context, were the production forces in China very different from other societies?

ii) while it is true to assert that scientific efforts and accomplishments are frequently a response to materialistic requirements of society, it would be a gross **mistake** to say that this is always possible or practical. Many social needs have remained unfulfilled for thousands of years. While countless examples can be quoted to support this, a very simple and obvious one may suffice. The human need for eye spectacles goes back in history probably as long as human life itself, but this great invention was only made by Europeans in the 13th century, after they learnt about light, its rays, reflection and diffraction from the Muslims.

Did this major invention come about as a result of a new need at the time, in relation to economic and materialistic circumstances of society? Or was it not the outcome of thinking processes that led to the perfection of that product when development matured to the required level?

Another instance which raises similar questions include the discovery in 13th century Europe of the phenomenon of magneticism, whereby magnetic needles could be used to guide sea vessels. When we remember that seaborne transport had been the primary routes of trade for many centuries previously, we could safely say that that event did not come a moment too soon. Romans, for instance, depended heavily on sea routes for their trade, but did not have the opportunity to discover the power of magnetic field in directing their ships, nor did their economic circumstances preclude them from such an opportunity. There is, however, some evidence to show that China had achieved a feet in this area, some 20 centuries prior to Europe.

It is also possible for science to *overtake* social needs, when relevant conditions are present. It is reported, for example, that steam power was discovered in the third century, that is ten centuries before any practical industrial applications could be made of that giant feet. It is true that steam power was not utilised when it was first thought of (i.e. third century), but here we are looking mainly at scientific knowledge , and any relevant links with social needs, as well as the progress of this knowledge and the conditions for it throughout history.

iii) Marxism has *confused* natural and pure science, on the one hand, with practical techniques, on the other. Practical industrial techniques normally emanate from ordinary experience and empirical trials that are conducted by business and skill-based people. These are arts that can be inherited, positively exploited in the course of production processes, and they usually grow in tandem with the needs of the forces of production.

On the other hand, pure experimental sciences have never been confined to the service of production methods. Thus, we find that pure science had, for along time, been moving on a separate path to that of practical down-to-earth techniques.

This is very evident over the period from the 16th to the 18th centuries. Techniques with practical leanings were born at around the 16th century, but actual incorporation of the pure sciences into these techniques did not begin until the 18th century. All this indicates that science has its own *independent* history, and it is not inevitably a reaction to the changing requirements of the production process.

iv) dependency of pure science on productive powers, whereby Marxists view the latter as the source that underpins the former and furnishes it with means for research. In fact, this relationship may be quite the *reverse* of what Marxism envisages, in the sense that advancements in science provide production with new avenues for development and sophistication.

The discovery of the microscope in the 17the century is but such instance, where a revolution was effected in productive methods, because a veil was lifted from a whole unknown world that was unavailable to mankind. But that wonderful instrument was nothing but a product of science; so was the discovery of the basic laws of light and how it reflects on lenses.

It is also necessary to note that science does not always require tools. There have been so many instances where scientific facts were far removed from the human eye, until sufficient interaction came about among/within scientific minds, so that such truths could be discovered and framed in special scientific notions. Perhaps the simple idea of the 'atmospheric pressure', which was developed back in the 17the century, can illustrate this. While the phenomenon itself had been known for centuries, it was left to Torricelli to elaborate it, through comparing the effects of pressure on water and mercury. This basic finding led to several significant discoveries.

3.2.3 Marxist Class Structure

An essential ingredient of Marxism is its concept of **class structure**. This notion is *unique* to Marxism, and fits in with its general method of looking at all social phenomena from an economic angle. It is from this general perspective that Marxists maintain that all societies are split into classes. The main dividing line among classes - according to Marxists - is the issue of property-ownership, as the owning class are dominant over those deprived of such an advantage.

This very point illustrates the skill and originality of Marxists, in explaining social phenomena within an essentially economic context. Yet, this skill has cost Marxists dearly, in that it forced them to become **unrealistic** in terms of their historical analysis. When we look at history, we do not **always** find that the ruling class are the owners of the means of production, while the ruled are non-owners.

More often than not, we see that it is the **circumstances** of each class which influence the economic conditions of its members. Effectively, this is the **reverse** of the Marxist notion, which regards economic realities as determining the class make-up of any society.

In all probability, when Marxism viewed economic circumstances as the basis of the class structure, it did not quite appreciate the logical consequence of that assertion. In effect, this Marxist hypothesis meant that people who were active in their areas of specialism, and who consequently became well-off, would necessarily attain social prominence - as members of a ruling class.

As we all know, this is very far from the truth! How can it be said that those who are active and successful in their fields, and who accomplish great economic gain, will rise to social prominence and become part of the governing elite? This situation may have held true in the case of capitalistic society during its development and maturity stages, but in only few other cases.

Some examples may illustrate this. In Roman society, rigid dividing lines were in place, to separate the nobles from all the rest, who included business-people, some of whom were wealthier than the nobles but without any of the latter's privileges, especially as far as governing the society is concerned.

Another example is the high social position enjoyed by the Samurai class in ancient Japanese society. That high standing was based on the ability of members of that class in using the sword and other horse-mounted arts, thus giving them a social position that was second only to feudalistic rulers.

The history of India makes clear that some 2000 years prior to the modern epoch of that semi-continent, a caste system was instituted by the Veda-Aryans who had invaded the country. That system was based on colour and blood, and in time the ruling class was itself split into two groups, namely the Kashatriya (warrior caste) and Brahman (priestly caste). All other castes (including merchants, artisans and property-owners) continued to be ruled by these two cast-systems. At the same time, indigenous tribes adhered to their religion and remained at the bottom of the social ladder, giving rise in the process to the class of 'untouchables'.

And, lastly, how are we to explain the setting up of the feudalistic order in western Europe as a result of Germanic conquest, by other than political-cum-military concepts? It is clear to all that those conquerors, who formed the ruling elite, did so not because of their belonging to the feudal social class, but by virtue of sheer military and political might . They later acquired large feudal possessions, due to their social advantages - based on military and political privileges - as conquerors who entered a vast region.   In effect, ownership became **consequence** of conquest and social class, rather than resulting in social class and government.

It is clear, therefore, that non-Marxist elements creep into the analysis of history of social stratification. Marxists have attempted to say that links do exist between the economic factor and various social considerations, whereby mutual repercussions and effects between the two are inevitable. But such attempts will simply demolish the whole concept of historic materialism as Marxists have expounded it.

In consequence, the Marxist edifice will come crumbling down, so much so that it becomes very much like any other theoretical explanation of history, with a relative emphasis on economic content - while admitting the contributions other variables in the making of history.

Another corollary of the Marxist doctrine of history and class struggle is that a rather artificial and **_unrealistic_** dividing line is drawn between those who own the means of production and others who do not. Within the latter would be included not simply factory workers, farm labourers, street sweepers etc., but also prominent members of the professions (e.g. doctors, accountants, engineers, company directors). On the other side of the divide, there will be not just the large capitalists, but very small business people as well.

As a result of all this, it is possible to draw *two* critical conclusions, these being:

First: it is possible for social class to exist even in the **absence** of property/ownership relationships. As has now become clear, such relationships are not the only grounds for the formation of social classes[5]. This in fact is the very thing that Marxists had feared, hence their emphasis on property/ownership as the *only* cause behind the class system, as well as their insistence on eradicating this ingredient under socialism.

Second: struggle within society (where it exists) does not simply reflect economic values, as determined through the distribution system in that society. Due to the complexities inherent in human societies, it is not merely the amount of income/wealth that determines social class, nor the type of income (e.g. profit received, wages, or salaries). Conflict lines within any society are drawn on the basis of other considerations as well.

3.2.4 Marxism and Natural Factors

A major defect of Marxist theory is the near neglect of physiological, psychological and physical factors, and the less than adequate appreciation of their role in history. In some cases, these factors have had a significant bearing on lives of individuals and social

---

[5] This is actually corroborated by the experience of the former Soviet Union, where it was declared that socialism had been accomplished, while wide differences among people continued to be widespread, in terms of pay levels, wealth, and social standing **(translator's comment)**.

progress, due to their influence on people and their private emotions and capabilities.

We all know of the historic role fulfilled by Napoleon Bonaparte, and the effects on Europe of his military talents and unique courage. The wobbliness of King Louis XV (15th), of France, was legendary, in that it allowed a single woman (Madam Pompadour) to push France to enter a seven-year war on the side of Austria, with catastrophic consequences. Then, there were the romantic exploits of the English King Henry VIII (8th), which led directly to the severance of the royal family, as well as England as a whole, from the Catholic faith.

There were also the effects of parental devotion that drove Muawiyah I (first)[6] to enlist loyalty to his incompetent son Yazid, so as to succeed him as Caliph of Muslims in the seventh century. That event unleashed a series of consequences in the Muslim world, and totally changed the course of history.

Would it be incorrect to maintain that human history would have been very different had any of these major events not taken place? Of course, these are but a tiny sample of critical junctures in human history, as there are many others beside. The effects of such human characteristics as resolve, wobbliness, lust, parental emotion, and others have been enormous on the currents of history. How is it possible, therefore, to relate all this to the state of production forces and economic circumstances?

It hardly possible to explain these characteristics away through the economic factor and production forces. Means of production and economic conditions are definitely not the factors that had moulded the particular temper of, say Louis XV. Circumstances permitting, that French king might have been assertive and strong-willed, as was Louis XIV (14th) or Napoleon. Quite clearly, the behaviour of the

---

[6] Muawiyah I (first) is regarded as the founder of the Amouyat epoch in the history of Muslims, which followed immediately the four major Caliphs who succeeded the Prophet (PBUH). Muawiyah was known to be a skilful politician, though his strategies and tactics were often far removed from orthodox Islamic teachings **(translator's comment)**.

former was the product of his particular temperament, that had been brought about through a certain physical, physiological and psychic make-up, which were an integral part of his special entity and particular personality.

Marxists may retort by claiming that the network of social relationships in France had been determined by the economic factor, and that network allowed Louis XV to influence history, through his unorthodox and feeble behaviour. The role fulfilled by that king was nothing but a product of the prevailing system at the time, which in turn was shaped and moulded by economic circumstances and the forces of production. In other words, the system of hereditary monarchy allowed Louis XV to become king, and thus affect through his actions the general movement of history.

But why was Louis XV deprived of adequate resolve? Does the explanation lie in the system of monarchy, or in natural variables that shaped the king's make-up and particular personality? In other words, three possibilities may be spelled out here, as follows:

a) France could have been a republic
b) France having a king with a wobbly personality
c) France having a king with a strong iron personality.

According to Marxist thought, the economic situation did not permit a republican system to exist in France, and thus the monarchical system was the chosen alternative. Even if this was sound reasoning, why should the king be so weak and easily influenced? In essence, there is no convincing explanation, except that offered by the laws of physics, physiology and psychology.

Nor is it proper to say - as some have - that the role of individuals in history is always minor and incidental. If one of the German scientists was able to develop the atom bomb earlier than the western Allies, would not this have changed the sequence of events in World War II, and consequently the course of history? The inability of

Adolf Hitler's regime to do this could not have been due to pure economic factors and the quality of the productive forces.

3.3.5 Marxism and Artistic Taste

Artistic taste is another social phenomenon that has been common to all ages and eras of history, irrespective of the nature of the system and production relationships. However, this important fact does not seem to have its rightful place within the general scheme of historical materialism.

No doubt, aesthetic taste has several aspects. One such aspect is when an artist paints an admirable portrait of a political leader or a military battle. We may thus enquire about the tools that this artist had utilised in perfecting his/her work, or may question the underlying motive behind the work. Yet, a third line of enquiry may seek to identify the reasons for our admiration and interest in the painting.

Marxists *may* respond to these three questions in the following manner:

a) the nature of method and tools employed by the painter hinge upon the state of the productive forces, and how developed they are.

b) in answering the second issue, Marxists would claim that art has invariably been utilised for the service of the ruling elite. As the governing class is essentially the product of the forces of production, then it is the nature of these forces again that are the ultimate arbiter and determinant of any piece of art.

c) an intriguing issue is set off by the third question. Why do we ordinary folks admire works of art and find them interesting and worthy of our attention? Can all this be explained by the nature of the productive forces and class-based interests which generate within us this admiration? Or is there a deep feeling in our conscious that craves for artistic excellence, regardless of the state of the productive forces or class-related considerations?

It is pertinent to note here that historical materialism imposes a verdict, which is imperative on Marxism to acquiesce to. This verdict explains artistic taste in terms of he productive forces and class-related interest, because the economic factor is considered to be at the root of all social phenomena.

However, this reasoning is fallacious. If the production forces bring about artistic taste, then the latter would have to change and develop as the former alters and progresses with the passage of time. But as we well know, ancient art remains just as worthy of admiration and interest as current works, if not more so.

Centuries-old aesthetic marvels are a source of much joy for people, who find such works immensely stimulating and highly praiseworthy, despite the passing of time, and regardless of social class, political system, creed, colour or religion. Is it not a common human essence which explains this phenomenon?

In this connection, Marx attempts to reconcile historical materialism with our admiration for ancient art, through claiming that the latter represents human childhood, in the same manner that any individual delights in recounting memories about one's childhood past, which is honest and devoid of complication and intrigue. But he does not tell us whether this enjoyment in childhood memories is an essential human trait or a changeable characteristic that develops and adjust with the economic factor.

And, why do we humans delight in Greek pieces of arts, and find them so fascinating? At the same time, why are we impressed in similar fashion by other aspects or phenomena of the ancient Greeks' primitive life, ideas and concepts, while all these also express human childhood?

And, what would Marx say about pure natural scenery, which have always been a source for satisfying the quest for beauty in men and women, since the beginning of human life? Why do we enjoy such scenic beauty, in much the same was as did our fathers and forefathers, no matter whether the individual is rich or poor, master or slave, feudalist or serf, capitalist or shopfloor worker? In fact, such scenery is not related to our feelings of free, unbounded and naive childhood, on the basis of which Marx explains our love of antiquated artefacts.

Is it not fair to deduce from all this that human enjoyment of art is not a question of being impressed with images from childhood? In actual fact, it is more to do with the essence of aesthetic art, which makes individuals of the slavery age overcome with similar emotions to that felt by people of the free world!

Finally, it is only fair to ask Engels to repent. As a main founder of historical materialism, he and his friend Marx, exaggerated the role of the economic factor in the history of mankind, and it is only proper for Marxists to come clean and admit their mistake in their pursuit of the materialistic notion of history.

~ *Chapter Four* ~

Detailed Aspects of Marxist Economics

When we look at Marxism in greater detail, it becomes necessary to start from the initial stages of history, which Marxists regard as the era of **primitive communism**. According to Marxist theory, human beings passed through a phase of early communism at the very beginning, and this contained within it the seeds of an antithesis.

The laws of dialectics stipulate that the antithesis will grow and become more powerful, and this -Marxists claim- was exactly what occurred then. So primitive communism was destroyed, and its very opposite – the slavery system – rose to prominence.

4.1   DID COMMUNIST SOCIETY EXIST?

Of course, a major question arises, as to whether primitive communism *actually* existed!   How can we ascertain this, through scientific evidence, since we are talking here about history long before any records began to be taken?

Marxists have attempted to overcome this difficulty, through observing certain currently existing communities that they labelled as *'primitive'* and thus viewed by them as worthy evidence in this regard.   As this evidence indicates that communism is the prevalent socio-economic system in such communities, Marxists inferred that all primitive societies had been characterised by a similar system.

But it is essential to note that Marxists had not actually visited those currently primitive societies, so as to directly collate information on them. Instead, such information as had been obtained came through other individuals, who had the opportunity to observe those communities at first hand. More seriously, Marxists only took note of the information that corresponded with their own theory, while branding all contravening evidence or data as perverted and false.

As a result, all Marxist research in this field tended to be selective, choosing that information which corroborated Marxist theory, and then the theory was judged on the basis of that shaky evidence. In lieu of that, the proper method was to take all available and objective data, and then measure the soundness of the theory on that basis.

Even if we acquiesce that the information obtained by Marxists regarding those so-called primitive societies are correct, a question mark can be raised about the extent to which those societies were actually primitive[1]. No concrete evidence could Marxists provide to support the contention that those societies were *in fact* primitive, in the scientific sense. An argument can be made out that those societies must have reached a certain level of development, and that their initial situation was much more primitive. Indeed, Marxist theory itself asserts that any society must develop through history, assuming quite firmly that no society can remain stuck to primitive or antiquated ways.

---

[1] The author refers to certain societies which were regarded by Marxists as primitive, including the Red Indian tribes prior to the discovery of North America, the Eskimos, and certain parts of Africa. **(Translator's Comment)**

4.2 AN EXPLANATION OF PRIMITIVE COMM-UNISM

The Marxist understanding of the epoch of primitive communism is that people then had to produce in a ***communal*** way. They had to group socially, in order to face nature, because humans were relatively weak, with little room for manoeuvre.

Ownership relationships had to be of the ***common-socialist*** type, as no private possession of the means of production could be tolerated. In essence, this was due to the common nature of the production process, and distribution among people was on the basis of equality.[2]

As forces of production were restricted in both quality and quantity (i.e. level of productivity), what could be produced (especially food and other essential items) had to be split equally. No other conceivable method could be imagined, because if anyone got a share larger than the others, then the result would be starvation for a certain section of the community.

In this way, then, Marxism explains the rational and main traits of primitive society where communism is supposed to had been practised. Yet, there is a glaring contradiction here, because individuals supposedly had the right to obtain their reasonable or adequate feeding, even if they were lazy or too feeble to work. According to Marxist ideology, needy people could enter other people's homes and help themselves to what they required of food and other essentials!

All this is based on research done on living conditions and culture patterns prevailing among Red Indian tribes, which were assumed to resemble closely the situation prevailing in primitive societies. The

---

[2] In ' The Origins of Private Property, the Family and the State', F Engels put forward the argument that only in the first forms of communal existence there were non-exploitive, non-oppressive relations, because social life and the direct struggle for survival were so immediately related, and the product of such work so immediately related to consumption, that no class differentiation was possible. See in this regard the following work :
John W Rees : 'The Algebra of Revolution' Routledge, 1998, Pages 120-121(note 61)

view was formed that in those societies (Red-Indian tribes), it was a major crime for anyone to withhold assistance from an individual who required help, and people who committed such acts would be ridiculed and frowned upon. But this means that it was possible for people to avoid work, yet obtain their basic requirements, though with some loss of dignity.

Such information on primitive communist societies seem to indicate that there was noticeable disparities in wealth and income during that epoch. Also, these supposed features of primitive societies point towards relative plenty in output, which would provide for the poor and infirm.

Why then was it necessary to divide the cake *equally*? And, how come that nobody would have thought of cheating and manipulating the distribution system to their own private advantage? There again, if people could abuse the system, but they refrained form such action, then we need to know the underlying reason(s) for such virtuous behaviour. These reasons may be found –perhaps – in the level of consciousness of primitive humans, and their practical attitude, while phenomena such as abuse and exploitation may have come about at subsequent stages, due to development and accumulation of human experience.

Moreover, what reasonable grounds could we find for the phenomenon that some people were too lazy to work but could still manage to stay alive? Does common participation in production entail the provision of essential items to those who did not contribute any effort? And if primitive people were eager to split the communal cake equally, so that nobody would starve, and thus deprive the community of their labour, why would they not allow the lazy to disappear? The loss of the latter would mean the cake would be split among fewer people!

4.3 ANTITHESIS OF PRIMITIVE COMMUNISM

Marxists would say that primitive communist society contained the seeds of its own destruction – right from the start. This **antithesis** was not class-based, because – by definition – a communist society would be classless. The contradiction, therefore, was due to the clash between communal ownership – on the one hand – and the forces of production, when these forces began to grow and develop, so much so that communal relationships became restrictive towards the continued improvement of those forces.[3]

Thus, the next question is why do communal relationships became such a hindrance? Marxists maintain that as productive forces develop, individual productivity would be enhanced, and surplus output would appear. The individual – or family – would be able to work less in order to feed, clothe and provide other essentials for themselves.

New social forces would be born, in order to utilise the surplus energies towards making additional output. As primitive communist society contained no appropriate apparatus for this purpose, it became imperative for a new set of relationships to develop. In essence, Marxists argue that the slavery system was the natural successor of primitive communism, as the former allowed for the extra energies to be utilised, and thus additional output to be made available to society.

The beginnings of slavery were to be found in the enslavement of families, who would be conquered through battle, by a tribe. Previously the vanquished would be annihilated by the victors, owing to the futility of keeping the former alive. But as the concept of

---

[3] According to F Engels, primitive communism rested on the undeveloped level of productive techniques. Only when production was able to provide a surplus, at least for some members of society, did the division of labour develop to the point where classes were formed and where there was a break between domestic and other labour …Only when the productive process advanced to the point where the surplus product was so great as to provide for a 'communism of abundance' rather than the original 'communism of scarcity' did a new socio-economic set-up arise. Ibid.

slavery took root, it became more logical and beneficial to enslave conquered individuals, as the latter would produce over and above the quantity of feeding they required.

In this manner - we are told - prisoners of war became slaves. Consequently, as slave-owners became very rich, they turned their attention towards members of their own tribes, so as to utilise the latter's labour in a similar fashion, opening the door towards the division of society into masters and slaves. On the back of such a system, production continued to advance both quantitatively and qualitatively.

When we look closely at all the above, we clearly find that it is a **human** issue, rather than a question of productive forces. Essentially, the development of productive forces was attained through human effort. In this context, the social aspect of work is unrelated to the growth and increased sophistication of productive forces.

In other words, whether people work under the umbrella of a slavery system or a liberal economy is neither here nor there. What is important is that the workforce make a determined and conscious decision to advance and develop; progress can be accomplished under either system. In fact, a well-founded case can be made in favour of the liberal regime, in that people here work for themselves, with the ability and urge to think freely and improve, while any additional output can be equally shared among individuals. In contrast, slaves have no freedom to think, and therefore cannot contribute towards progress and development.

It is, therefore, only proper to infer that the developmental growth of the productive forces could not have hinged on the institution of slavery. Instead, that growth had much to do with better work input-both qualitative and quantitative. So, why did working people double their efforts *via* the slavery system, rather than through the free and individually-based enterprise system?

The answer to this question probably lies in the inclination of humans to do as *little* work as possible. When confronted with two work options, people tend to take the less onerous, unless they are forced on the harder path. This tendency is an essential human **trait**, not necessarily connected to the type of productive methods utilised.

This innate desire among humans to lessen the amount of effort exerted has had its fair share in moulding societies. In fact, it could be viewed as largely responsible for the rise of the slave-dependent system, as this system saves effort for the master, while reducing costs and maximising rewards. We can, therefore, say that it was *not* the forces of production that gave birth to slavery. Rather, it facilitated the move to such a system, while the crucial human make-up was the basic culprit.

An analogy may clarify this point. A sword is given to a person, who then uses this weapon to murder another person. Here, the real cause of the murder is the grudge inside the murderer towards the victim, while the sword itself is only an accessory, or an ancillary tool in the whole incident.

It is important to note here that Marxists have remained silent over another factor, which could have played a prime role in the withering of primitive communism, and the transfer to the slave-master set-up. Primitive communism might have led to laziness on the part of many individuals, rather than performing their proper role in production and development.

Marxists have ignored this important problem associated with communism, and the impact it had on dismantling the system, leading eventually to the enslavement of the inactive by the vigorous and fittest. On reflection, however, this Marxist standpoint is understandable.

Any admission that communism leads to laziness and dependency would diagnose the genuine and fundamental deficiency of such a system. By their psychic and organic nature, humans would not find communism a practical and viable system. All available evidence, from the beginning of human existence on Earth through the experiences of Russia and other socialist countries, are nothing but a living proof of the basic nature of people, their motives, and inner feelings.

4.4   SLAVERY-BASED SOCIETY

Slavery-based society is the second major phase of development is human history, according to historic materialism. It is during this stage that social classes come out in the open, and glaring contradictions arise between masters and serfs. In one form or another, this state of affairs (i.e. the class system) is still with us till the present day.

A major question can be posed here: how did some people manage to become masters, while others had to accept the lowly status of being serfs? And, had it not been possible for some individuals to switch roles?

Marxists have a clear and ready answer to this: each of the two main sections within slavery had to perform a specific and pre-designated role, that was delineated by the economic factor and production setting. Those who became masters were wealthy people, and consequently capable of committing others to the bond of slavery. But the intriguing point here is this: how could these people *acquire* wealth, while everybody were living in a primitive communist society, where individuals were equal?

A *two-pronged* reply is given by Marxists to this point, as follows:

First: those who came to assume prominent positions, during primitive communism, would abuse their position to gain and accumulate wealth. This applies to military chiefs, clergy and other community leaders, who would siphon part of the communal ownership for their own personal ends, in a gradual fashion, so as to form an exclusive aristocracy. The less fortunate would lose in the process, and necessarily fall, in a piecemeal manner, under the sphere of influence of the better off.

Second: in some cases, prisoners of war were transferred to being slaves, thereby enabling certain individuals to profit from this process. This heightened the degree of inequality, and enhanced social contradictions and resultant conflicts, as wealthy individuals possessed the means for enslaving members of their own tribes who became debtors or lost wealth.

Both of the above explanations fly in the face of historic materialism. The first explanation regards the political factor as the more fundamental, while relegating economics to a secondary role, due to the assumption that community leaders found themselves in prime positions prior to acquiring wealth. Wealth, therefore, followed the assumption of prime position, rather than *vice versa* as Marxist ideology asserts.

The second explanation, which purported to rationalise the disparities in wealth, does not stand a better chance than the first. It assumes that masters were able to enslave prisoners of war, before they could do the same to members of their clans. But what gave those very individuals the opportunity to treat prisoners of war in that way? Marxists have shunned this critical question, because there is *no* adequate explanation within the context of the forces of production.

In fact, the real explanation can be found within the realm of humanity. People differ in their capabilities, whether physical, cognitive, or military. Very often, individuals are borne with particular characteristics, abilities and endowments, which in turn spawn their actual conditions and environment, in terms of psychology, physiology, natural surroundings etc.

4.5   THE FEUDAL SOCIETY

Due to certain critical contractions, the slavery system is supposed to have given way to the feudal set-up. Those contradictions resulted from the inherent rivalries within slavery, and the qualitative growth of the forces of production. In consequence, slave-based relationships became a hindrance to development and growth, from two aspects:

Firstly: the slavery system opened the way for masters to abuse their subjects in a savage and inhuman fashion, particularly in the field of production. Consequently,, many slaves perished in the process, and this left a negative impact on production and society's welfare in general.

Secondly: the slavery system had the effect of pushing most free men and women (e.g. peasants and craftspeople) to become slaves. Thus, society lost much of the non-slave soldiers, through whom incursions and invasions of other societies could be undertaken; therefore new waves of slaves could not be acquired

As a result, and because of the above two factors, society came to suffer substantial reductions in productive resources, both due to internal wastage and the inability to import additional numbers through battle and taking new prisoners. Therefore, a sharp conflict of interest came to the surface, between the system itself and those benefiting from it, on the one hand, and the forces of production, who were eager to develop and improve. The product of that conflict was the building of the feudal structure on the ashes of the slavery system.

Three essential points are ignored by Marxism in this exposition. **First**, if we look for example, at the transformation of Roman society from slavery into feudalism, we find that this was **not** revolutionary in nature, emanating from the phenomenon of class struggle – as required by the dialectic nature of historic materialism.

In the **second** place, this major transformation in society was not preceded by development in the forces of production, as required by Marxist theory, which presumes that the means of production are the ultimate instrument in moving history[4]. And **thirdly**, the economic situation was afflicted by a general setback, and therefore did not exhibit an advance or an improvement, to provide a profile of integrated sequence of development and advance.

All the above indicates that the destruction of slavery and building of the feudal system had not proceeded in accordance with Marxist ideology, because the economic factor does seem to have been influential in the overall process of change. The above three points can now be investigated more closely.

A)   Non-revolutionary Transformation

If we take Roman society, no class-related revolution was experienced in the transformation from slavery to feudalism. Nor did that transformation take place at a precise point in history. All this contradicts historical materialism, which contemplates as essential such a revolt, in attaining change form any historical phase to the next. While dialectical reasoning accepts the notion and practice of gradual change, any such piecemeal changes are viewed to accumulate into major qualitative pushes at the opportune time.

It is clear, therefore, that in the case of Roman society, the dialectic doctrine of historic materialism remained inoperative, because no instantaneous revolution took place to effect the transfer to the feudal system. Instead, the change – as Marxists have confirmed – was brought about by the masters themselves, who began to free many of their slaves. They divided their large land holdings into smaller allotments and handed out these to their erstwhile slaves, after they realised that the slavery system did not secure their interests.

---

[4] It is fair to assume here that the author continues to refer to Roman society and its transformation from slavery to feudalism. **(Translator's Comment)**

In this manner, the owning class transformed society gradually to the feudal phase. It is also intriguing to note that while historical materialism expected revolutions at the prime defining moments, such events tended to happen long before the final collapse of the system.

In the case of Sparta, the campaign by slaves erupted some four centuries before Christ, when thousands of slaves gathered near the city attempting to storm it, and the city's leaders had to request military assistance from neighbouring cities, while the revolt could not be eradicated until several years later.

Likewise, there was the slave uprising led by Spartacus some 70 years before Christ, where tens of thousands of slaves took part, and the whole edifice of the Roman Empire was threatened. This movement actually preceded the birth of the feudal system by several centuries, a fact that indicates that social contradictions had not by then ripened to a sufficient degree; nor did the development of the productive forces reach the required level. Instead, that popular movement drew its strength and inspiration from increasing awareness about oppression, plus a distinct ability in the interrelated areas of mobilisation, military action and mass leadership. The conclusion, therefore, is that it is wrong to rationalise each and every change as social expression of the pressing needs of the forces of production.

In the words of F Engels 'so long as a mode of production is still in the rising stage of its development, it is enthusiastically welcomed by even those who come off worst from its corresponding mode of distribution. This was the case with the English workers in the beginning of large-scale industry. So long as this mode of production remains normal for society, there is general contentment with the distribution, and if objections to it begin to be raised, these come from within the ruling class itself'.[5]

---

[5] Friedrich Engels: " Herr Eugen Duhring's Revolution in Science (*Anti-Duhring*)" Lawrence & Wishart, London, Pg.170 (no date given).

But how, on this basis, can we explain the slave uprisings that preceded the transformation of slavery into feudalism by several centuries? And if change comes about as a consequence of the floundering of the production system (rather than some psychological or practical difficulties faced by individuals), then why did those masses of slaves expressed their collective anger while the slavery system was – for the most part – running fairly smoothly?

B)   No Renovation of Productive Forces

Marxism believes that social patterns follow the type of production system in force: each pattern of production entails a specific kind of social set-up and ownership patterns. But when we look at production patterns, we find that they remained virtually the same under both slavery and feudalism. No development or renovation in production could be discerned to have occurred, as slavery gave way to feudalism. In fact, prevailing productive methods over that epoch were mainly in agriculture and manual labour. The slave-related social framework vanished before the occurrence of any basic change in productive forces – and this is contrary to Marxist assertions.

On the other hand, we do find that various patterns of production had been dealt with, and transcended, by the forces of production, without any clear change in social relationships. As Marxists have concurred, primitive humans made use of natural stones and stony tools, then fire was discovered; axes and lances were made. As a result, the forces of production developed, leading to the evolution of metal instruments, bows and arrows; subsequently farm production developed, and then animal output.

All these significant changes in production patterns took place without any major transformation in the social set-up and general relationships. According to Marxist thought, all those alterations in production methods and patterns proceeded during primitive society and while communism was the prevailing system.

We can thus affirm the conclusion that it is possible for production patterns to alter with the social set-up remaining virtually the same. It is equally possible, as in the case of the transfer from slavery to feudalism, that social change might come about while the production system is standing still. How, then, may we accept the concept that each social pattern is consequent upon a specific production set-up?

Is it not preferable for Marxists to assert that any social system is a result of practical ideas elaborated by people throughout their social experiences of contacts with one another? Also, would it not be better to maintain that production patterns are spawned via scientific processes, and associated contemplation, that people experience in their interface with natural resources in this world?

While natural experiments are generally short-term in nature, it is possible for these experiments to accumulate quickly. Conversely, social phenomena embody history of whole societies, and therefore practical ideas in this sphere must by necessity progress rather slowly. The upshot of all this is that it is quite reasonable to expect social change to be slower than alterations in production patterns.

C)   Imperfect Economic Situation

The slavery framework was unhelpful for the development of production – we are told - and therefore it was brushed aside to make way for feudalism. But were feudal conditions more appropriate for developing and polishing production techniques? And, did that transformation enable the economic framework, and in consequence the whole human trail following, to advance on an ever-rising curve, as required by the Marxist interpretation of history?

In fact, none of that happened, as evidenced by the economic conditions of Roman society. During the slavery phase of the Roman Empire, doors were opened ajar for high-level economic development, where commercial capitalism grew spectacularly, especially in certain parts of that Empire.

It is clear that commercial capitalism is a relatively advanced mode of economic system, hence indicating that the Romans had attained a reasonably high degree of economic sophistication, pushing heir society high up the ladder, compared with primitive and closed economies, or the so-called 'economics of the parlour'. All this gave fillip to trade among nations during Roman times, due notably to the construction of roads and protection of maritime routes, in addition to buoyant internal trade, i.e. within various parts of the Empire. It is well established, for instance, that Italy was renowned for its house-wares all over the world.

The following question, therefore, poses itself: why did economic conditions (as embodied in commercial capitalism) not continue their march towards improvement and perfection? Why was it not possible for commercial capitalism to advance towards industrial capitalism (as happened in the middle of the 18th century), since the merchant class did posses sufficient capital, while the masses of free people were ready and eager for such a transformation?

This means that the material conditions for taking society a significant step further on the ladder of advancement were available. So, if these conditions were enough, why did the supposed advance not come about?

In fact, when the feudal system came into existence, the Roman Empire witnessed the virtual ending of commercial capitalism and its final demise. Each major landowner became a little state into himself, with well-defind borders and a virtually manor-based closed economy. Manor-sufficiency ruled supreme, whereby output of farm produce and other craft-based items was viewed enough to sustain the economic life of each such community. Consequently, trade diminished, commercial capitalism receded, and the whole society shrank to a parlour-style basic economy.

4.6   RISE OF CAPITALISTIC SOCIETY

And finally, feudalism started receding, after it became a major
problem and a handicap to production.   Historical developments
produced a way out, in the form of **capitalism** that had risen as a
social phenomenon, threatening the feudal system. Capitalism was
the exact antithesis of feudalism, and the former had grown in the
latter's shadow, until conditions advanced sufficiently for complete
victory to be attained.

In his analysis of capitalism, Marx gives a great deal of attention to
what he calls the **'primary accumulation of capital'**.   This is
definitely a notion of much significance, as its understanding is
essential for analysing the historical existence of capitalism. On the
rubbles of the feudalistic structure, a new class of capital-owning
industrialists breeds and grows, utilising in the process their own
financial resources and employing wage-earning labourers.   It is
necessary, however, to assume that certain factors had made it
possible for such financial accumulation to take place.[6]

A given class of people must have been able to accumulate wealth,
while a great mass of workforce must have been gathered. What,
then, are the underlying factors which made all this possible?   In
other words, what is the mystery of the initial capitalistic
accumulation, which gave rise to the capitalist class, vis-à-vis another
class of wage-earners?

In his attempt to deal with this issue, Marx starts with an exposition
of a traditional standpoint in political economy, which had been
claiming that certain individuals could acquire special advantages by
virtue of their intelligence, self-discipline and financial astuteness.
Those individuals would thus be able to set aside some part of their
income, so as to build-up a viable amount of capital.

---

[6] See in this regard the following work:
C J Arthur : ' Marx's Capital', Lawrence & Wishart, London, 1992, Pg..376-378

In spelling out this viewpoint, Marx utilised his usual cynicism in critically exposing, and even ridiculing, any ideas different from his own, reaching the final assertion that saving *by itself* was not an adequate reason for explaining the process of initial accumulation of capital, which made it possible for the new capitalist class to assert itself. He added that it was imperative in this context to look into the essential ingredients of the capitalist system and dwell into its complex mysteries.

For this purpose, Marx used fully his unique and impressive ability of expression, along with his total control of idioms, in trying to corroborate his viewpoint. In his view, capitalism presents us with a special type of relationship, one between the capitalist and the wage-earner, where the first owns the means of production, while the latter surrenders all claims to ownership of fruits of his/her labour.

In the context of the production system, the labourer possesses nothing, barring his/her energy to work. On the other had, the capitalist owns all relevant integrating ingredients: materials, tools, machines, and the ability to pay employees. The wage-earners' standpoint towards this system stems from their lack of any means of production, or the ability to acquire those means – quite unlike the capitalist.

Capitalism, therefore, is based fundamentally and squarely on this separation between the wage-earner and means of production, despite the fact that the former is the one who interfaces with the latter, in order to effect the specified output. And, this separation has been essential throughout history, in order for capitalistic systems to exist. The existence of a capitalist system entails – by necessity – that the means of production had been taken over or seized by capitalists, after they were in the hands of the actual (small-scale) producers.

It is thus essential for commercially-oriented capitalists to be owning the bulk of the means of production. The process embodying a clear division between producer and property-owner, with the latter being the commercially-minded capitalists, is therefore the key for attaining the initial stage of capital accumulation. This initial stage came about through several methods, including armed acquisition, deportation, stealing and violence. This indicates, therefore, that such things as good sense, self discipline, astute personal economic management, piety and intelligence had little role in this process - quite contrary to what traditional political economic thinkers had imagined!

An important question can be raised here: how successful was Marx in this explanation of the initial accumulation of capital? In fairness, it can be said quite categorically that Marx had not intended to morally discredit capitalism, by showing that it was based on theft, embezzlement and low morals, because he regarded the system as a normal advance forward in history.

In his view, when capitalism came about, it did so at the historically appropriate juncture, and that it contributed towards the natural futuristic development of mankind. When it evolved, the capitalist system coincided with prevailing concepts, morals and culture, as all these were - and still are - the product of economic conditions and the relevant state of the productive forces. If and when these very forces require the institution of the capitalist system, then naturally all value judgements and mannerism of the corresponding era will adjust accordingly, Marx tells us.

If we now turn our attention to the evaluation of Marx's analysis, we find first that he made a skilful and eloquent effort to put across his viewpoint, employing in the process first-rate semantics. He noted quite astutely that production relationships under capitalism hinge upon the availability of a workforce who did not possess the means of production, while at the same time had the ability to operate those means and utilise them to produce the requisite output.

But he also claimed that the trading-capitalist class acquired wealth and the means of production through sheer force and devious methods. In effect, Marx's claims boil down to the assumption that the working class did previously own the means of production, but they were forcefully deprived of them. This adds a novel element which was not present in the pure analysis regarding the establishment of the capitalist system.

Four prime comments can now be made about all this:

Firstly: this description does not hold true with regard to some societies where capitalism was built on the ashes of feudalism, as was the case in Germany, where many feudalists had taken the initiative to directly build factories and mange them; they financed them from their feudalistic earnings. It was not necessary, therefore, for the transfer from feudalism to capitalism to be effected through a new process of confiscation or forceful acquisition, so long as the feudalists themselves were ready to be involved in capitalist production, by utilising their own wealth.

In similar fashion, the transfer of commercial profits into industrial capitalism did not occur according to Marxist prescriptions. This was quite clear in the case of the Italian trading city-republics of Venice, Florence and Genoa, as well as in other cases.

A class of traders existed in all these cases, prior to the appearance of industry, i.e. before the setting up of the capitalist system in its industrial form, the roots of which Marx was eager to discover. Craft workers used to work for themselves; traders were purchasing the resultant output and making in the process a great deal of profits through commerce with the East, as these trade routes flourished strongly after the crusader wars.

The role of these traders strengthened enormously, due to their attaining monopolistic position in that trade, through certain special understandings with local rulers, who had sovereign power in regions such as Syria and Egypt. In consequence, the profits of those traders multiplied, and thus were able to eradicate the influence of the land owners, so as to establish large manufacturing plants. These units in turn - and through sheer commercial competition - replaced small craft-based industries, thus giving rise to capitalist production or industrial capitalism.

Secondly: the Marxist viewpoint is not sufficient to solve the problem, because it simply asserts that the process of history led to the workers being deprived of their means of production, so that these means would be concentrated in the hands of traders, who created the initial process of capitalist accumulation. Marxism, however, does not explain to us how members of a given class came to possess the power to subjugate others through violence, so as to deprive producers of their means of production through sheer force.

Thirdly: even if we concede that the power to subjugate others did come about, and we avoid the need to rationalise it, this is hardly an acceptable component within the overall framework of Marxist ideology. In essence, it is not an economic explanation, and does not fit comfortably with other elements making up the totality of Marxism.

How did Marx allow himself to explain the phenomenon of initial capital accumulation through violence and subjugation, which are not really economic ingredients? In fact, Marx could be laying himself open to criticism, by using such logic to expound the foundation of capitalism. As such, he admitted that the class system did not have a pure economic essence.

It would have been much better for Marx - and much in accord with historic materialism - to accept the traditional standpoint to rationalise the appearance of the capitalist class. That standpoint was on the receiving end of his ridicule and derision, but would in fact have provided a rationalisation nearer to the economic nature of events and actual phenomena.

Lastly: all that Marx gives by way of historical evidence to underpin his hypothesis of forceful deprivation is drawn from England only, showing how large English landowners resorted to depriving peasants of their lands, which were transformed to pasture. The hapless farmers were sacked and made jobless and homeless; they consequently found their way to the markets of the nascent bourgeoisie. In essence, therefore, those were actions to deprive farmers of their lands for the benefit of feudalists, rather than craftsmen of their means of production for the sake of the merchant class.

Tens of pages in Marx's *Capital* are filled with accounts of those violent events, through which landowners deprived farmers of their farmlands, paving the way for the upcoming capitalist system. However, Marx confined himself mainly to occurrences which had taken place in England, indicating that the real underlying reason for those actions was the landowners' wish to transform their farmlands to animal pasture.

As a result, the feudalists felt that they had superfluous farmers whom they had no need for. But why did the feudalists identify this sudden requirement to change the use of their land-holdings? Based on Marx's writings, C J Arthur points out that the "prelude of the revolution that laid the foundation of the capitalist mode of production was played in the last third of the fifteenth century and the first decade of the sixteenth century. A mass of free proletarians was hurled on the labour market by the breaking up of the of the bands of feudal retainers ..In insolent conflict with king and Parliament, the great feudal lords created an incomparably larger proletariat by forcible driving of the peasantry from the land, to which the latter had the same feudal right as the lord himself, and by the usurpation of the common lands.."[7]

This answer has a special historical importance, to which Marx did not pay enough attention. It means, in effect, that industrial production had flourished, in both England and Belgium. Capitalist commerce also expanded, in both wool products and other general items, with the advent of large markets for those goods.

---

[7] Op. cit.pg.366

All this handed a valuable opportunity to English feudalists to take stock of the situation, through adapting their farmland, so as to produce and sell wool to industrial plants. They were prompted to compete in conquering world markets for wool, as English wool had at that time certain features which put it at the forefront, as the main material in manufacturing high-quality woollen textiles.

It is clear from all this that the prime factors regarded by Marx as the historic pillars, on which capitalist society in England was founded, were not in the main related to the feudalist system. On the basis of the dialectical nature of historical materialism, it was not the feudalist system which produced the contradictions that destroyed it; nor was it the feudalist relationships that created those peculiar conditions. In reality, the true reason emanated from the high momentum of woollen textile production, and the buoyancy of commerce in this field.

Commercial capitalism encouraged large landowners to sack farmers and push them towards industrial towns. The new social relationships did not actually come about from contradictions within the feudalist system. Rather, the new socio-economic structure and associated relationships were influenced by the general prevailing environment, instead of being merely the result of contradiction in the former feudalist system.

In retrospect, Marx realised that forceful acquisition of assets by feudalists could not stand as the basis of initial wealth accumulation for industrial capital. He therefore made a new attempt to deal with this issue in a subsequent part of his book *'Das Capital'*. Here, he was not content to explain wealth accumulation in terms of commercial or usurious capitalism, which led to enormous wealth accumulation among the merchant and financier class. He explained, in addition, that the discovery of areas where deposits of gold and silver existed paved the way for the enslavement of indigenous inhabitants, ushering thereby the dawn of capitalism.

Thus once more, Marx endeavoured to explain the evolution of capitalist society through the use of force, conquest and colonialism, despite the fact that these were not by nature Marxist elements. They were not economic ingredients, expressing - as they do - political and military power. In fact, it can be argued that a contradiction arises here, because Marx insists that **force** is an 'economic factor'.

This assertion can be viewed as an attempt to square the circle, and break from the predicament. This is a glaring attempt to give the economic factor a very broad connotation, which would enable it to encompass virtually all factors that are needed in the analytic process.

While Marx is politically and morally correct in his objections to the use of force to institute capitalism in England, he cannot be supported in his conclusion that such immoral and obnoxious means are necessary to attain the transition to capitalism. Marx's assertion is based on the experience of England alone. When we look at the experiences of other nations, we do not necessarily find similar conditions, such as a rampant colonialist drive involving all types of criminal activities in various parts of the globe, as well as actions to deprive craftsmen of their means of production.

In 13th century Italy, capitalist production was set up, whereby many capitalist organisations were established, where thousands of wage-earners worked to produce a wide variety of goods. These were marketed in many countries, on behalf of capitalist landowners. Absent, however, were the symptoms which came to the surface in England during the 15th and 16th centuries, and which were looked at deeply by Marx.

A further example is provided by the Japanese experience. Japan's capitalist production started in the 19th century, whereby the whole society began moving from feudalism to the mould of industrial capitalism. It is plain that Japan was sunk deep into feudalism, when her nation were shockingly woken up to the soundings of bells heralding danger signals, and threatening the country with grave consequences. The first glaring salvo in this connection took place in the year 1853, when the US navy landed on Japanese shores, and began negotiating with the military authorities to agree bilateral protocols, thus alerting the Japanese to the possibilities of an economic invasion, which might lead to colonialism and destruction of the country.

As a result, Japanese leaders came to the view that virtually the only realistic option was to industrialise the country, establishing in the process a system of industrial capitalism, and following a path similar to that previously adopted by European nations. Major landowners participated in this strategy, and enormous efforts were exerted to bring about an industrial revolution in the country, so as to upgrade Japan to the standard of the main capitalist economies.

The land-owing aristocracy made strenuous strides, and co-operated fully with government authorities, in a loyal and selfless fashion, facilitating the transformation of the country to the industrial age. In the process, a class of traders and skilful people grew rapidly.

Members of this latter class were previously at the bottom of the social ladder. They used their newly-found wealth and influence to ease the peaceful break-up of the feudal system. A time came in 1871 when top landowners conceded the inevitable, and agreed to relinquish their age-old privileges. In return, the Japanese government compensated them for their land, via State securities issued to them. For the most part, therefore, everything proceeded amicably and peacefully, leading finally to the spectacular rise of industrial Japan.

Does all this resonate with the concepts of historic materialism and Marxist explanations of history? Marxists emphasise that change from one historical phase to another must go through a process of revolution, because small piecemeal changes lead to prime spontaneous pushes forward. But as has become quite evident, the Japanese transformation from feudalism to capitalism occurred peacefully, whereby major landowners capitulated and gave up their traditional status, saving the country a fateful upheaval such as the French revolution of 1789.

Moreover, Marxism regards as imperative that all evolution is the outcome of class struggle: one class stands for evolution; another opposed to it. However, the Japanese experience has shown that the whole society took a united stand for industrial development and modern capitalism. Even members of the land-owning aristocracy did not deviate from this common strategy, as they concurred - with all others - that the destiny of the country depended on modernisation and industrial development.

Marxism also views capitalist accumulation, which underpins the establishment of industrial capitalism, as the consequence of violent actions, invasions and forceful acquisition, instead of resulting through methods characterised by **'honest romance'**, as Marx would call them. Once again, the historical facts of Japan prove the very opposite of all this, as capitalist accumulation in that country did not go through violent or colonialist means.

Nor did small Japanese producers endure the misfortune or agony of forceful acquisition of their productive possessions. Instead, the new system was a product of activities in which all sections of society participated, including organs of the State and political groupings. A national bourgeoisie class was created, as a result of those ideological and political activities, rather than as a power-class which put together elements of the overall ideological and political climate that suited its purposes.

4.7 FUNDAMENTALS OF CAPITALISM

When an account of capitalist fundamentals is spelled out in accord with historical materialism, this in effect brings out the economic face of Marxism. Marxist economics glitters in its main characteristics through a study of capitalism, more than it does through looking at any other epoch of history.

Marxists have undertaken deep analysis of capitalist society and associated economic conditions, detailing the general framework of the system and its fundamentals, in line with the dictate of historical materialism. The result has been an emphatic viewpoint of what lies at the core of capitalism, especially the contradictions that should - supposedly - lead to final destruction of the system.

In his study of the essence of capitalist society and bourgeois principles of political economy, Marx began by analysing the concept of value in the process of exchanging goods and services in the economy. This concept was central within the context of a free market economy, and was the prime focus of attention from other economists - Marx's contemporaries and predecessors alike. As a result, Marx's analytic theory of value became the centrepiece of his overall theoretical structure.

In fact, Marx did not make a major contribution to the theory of value, but accepted the traditional theory that had previously been developed by David Ricardo. This theory says that human labour is the essence of value in the process of exchange. In other words, the value of any product made through human effort is assessed via the amount of labour embodied in it, and therefore the value of any item hinges on this criterion. Hence, the value of a product that requires one hour of labour should be half that of an item needing two hours.

This critical theory was the starting point for both Ricardo and Marx, in their analytic study of the working of capitalist economics. In fact, both Ricardo and Marx were preceded in this regard by other economists and thinkers who looked at this idea and directed attention towards it. Among these are the English philosopher John Locke, and the Scottish philosopher -cum-economist Adam Smith, who is often referred to as the father of classical free-market economics.

While Smith considered the above-mentioned theory of value in a rather limited and narrow fashion, a more detailed and comprehensive treatment was afforded by Ricardo, who believed quite firmly that labour was the general basis of value. What Marx did was to frame the theory in the context of his own particular ideology, adding certain clarifications and Marxist elements.

When Ricardo believed that labour was the basis of value, he was quick to realise that where monopoly held sway, it was possible for market value to be a multiple of its level in a competitive setting, where the forces of supply and demand would operate in a normal manner. For this reason, Ricardo adhered strongly to perfect competition, as a necessary condition for value to reflect labour content. Marx's view was pretty similar, recognising fully that the theory would not hold under monopoly.

Ricardo noted that people vary in their efficiency and productivity. One hour of labour from a vigilant and active worker would have a much higher outcome than the same from a slow uncaring soul. Ricardo dealt with this problem by presuming that for every type of craft or skill, there would be an acceptable standard of efficiency, and this standard may differ from one society to another[8].

After developing the theory of value, Ricardo realised that he had left out certain essential elements that helped to shape value, such as land and capital. He therefore developed his new theory of **land rent**, which caused a revolution in thinking on that topic. This theory attempted to prove that land did not contribute to the making of value, when perfect competition existed.

Pre-Ricardo economists were prone to the belief that land rent was a natural gift, that came about through a combination of human effort and land use, so as to result in agricultural production and the surfacing of value in the normal process of exchange within an economy. By implication, this meant that labour was *not* the only basis for value.

---

[8] In modern management theory and practice, this is referred to as the **standard time**, which is the average time taken by an operative with average skill to produce one unit, e.g. an average-skill assembly worker would assemble an electric motor in 10 minutes, indicating thereby that his normal productivity is 6 units per hour. **(Translator's Comment)**

It was, therefore, incumbent upon Ricardo to refute this explanation of land rent, so as to underpin his theory of value with a supporting explanation. He did that by interpreting land rent as the ***consequence of monopoly***, stressing that it would not appear under perfect competition. Landlords who had access to fertile land could reap special reward in the form of **rent**. The clear thesis here is that such rent was the product of a monopoly situation, as others had to content themselves with using less fertile plots of land.

With regard to capital, Ricardo expressed the standpoint that this factor was nothing more than a ***gathering*** action, saved in the form of tools, machines etc., so as to be utilised to bring about output. He believed that it was ***not*** necessary to view capital as an independent factor in creating value. A piece of equipment needs one hour to produce, and would then be utilised to make a further product that required two labour hours. The total time expended on this latter product would then be three hours. All this boils down to the conclusion that labour was the only solid basis determining value.

It might have followed from this that Ricardo would condemn or repudiate capitalist profit, but in fact nothing of the kind happened. He believed it reasonable for the price of any item to be determined in such a fashion as to yield a net return to capital-providers, arguing that the latter had to be compensated for the time-span that lapses between investment and the actual sale of products. Implicitly, therefore, Ricardo recognised the role of time as a factor in creating value. This represented another qualification on Ricardo's assertion that labour was the only basis for value, and may be construed as inability on his part to adhere in an orthodox way to his original theory.

When Marx came along and looked at non-labour factors of production, he noted Ricardo's analysis, but incorporated in it concepts of his own, some of which were rather radical. On the one hand, Marx studied Ricardo's theory of land rent and approved it, distinguishing in the process between ***differential*** rent - as set out by Ricardo - and ***absolute*** rent. The latter term was used by Marx to indicate a general return on land, resulting from natural monopoly, and the fact that only a limited area of land was available.

On the other hand, however, Marx lambasted Ricardo for recognising the need for capitalist **profit**. Using his own **value added** theory, he strongly criticised Ricardo for admitting the rationale of capitalist profit. The theory of added value can indeed by viewed as crucial within the totality of theoretical structure built by Marx.

4.8   MARX'S METHODOLOGY

In developing his concept of value, Marx starts by differentiating between value *in use* and value *in exchange*. A bed, spoon and a loaf of bread are products having values in usage, due to the actual utility rendered by each of these items.   In contrast, when the producer of any such item exchanges it for something else - be it money or another product/service - the good will attract a given value within the process of exchange.

While the practical value of a wooden bed and a gentleman's suit may be quite different, their market value (i.e. price) may be similar. Such a similar market value may be the only significant element in common between these two goods, thus expressing the amount of labour content deployed in each of them, which - according to Marxist thinking - need to be equal or nearly equal.

In essence, therefore, it is the **amount of labour** that determines the intrinsic value of any item, which ought to be equal or similar to the price in the open market. However, it is perfectly possible for these two (i.e. market price and intrinsic value) to differ, due to the normal operation of the forces of supply and demand, which can push market prices up or pull them down.   Yet, intrinsic value will constrain the operation of supply and demand, so as to prevent price from deviating too widely from that value.   The price of a handkerchief can certainly be increased abnormally at times of high demand, but would seldom - if ever - reach the market price of a motorcar.

Intrinsic value is, therefore, a solid basis for determining value; value is shaped by the volume of work embodied in the product. Also, the price of any item is a market reflection of that product's intrinsic value. Forces of supply and demand exert a secondary influence on market price, depending on how competitive is the marketplace, and whether monopoly is prevalent.

Marx noted - as did Ricardo before him - that this law of value does not apply to situations of monopoly. Under these circumstances, value would be determined through supply and demand, where the monopolist has a field day[9]. A similar scenario would arise in many cases of artistic or cultural production, such as a painting by a well-known artist, or an antiquated document with history extending to hundreds of years. Such an item would fetch a high market price, owing to its aesthetic or historical significance and despite the limited amount of labour expended on it.

For this reason, Marxists have declared that the validity of their labour-based law of value **depends** on two things:

a)   existence of complete(or **perfect**) competition, thus exempting monopoly situations.

b)   product made through social production, effected always via ordinary or **social labour**, thus exempting individual or special output, such as an artistic painting.

A crucial element in this Marxist analysis is worthy of note here. In his analysis and exploration of the theory of value, Marx adopted a purely **abstract** method, that was far removed from the factual environment and economic realities. Perhaps, it was for this reason,

---

[9] The implication here is that the monopolist firm would limit supply, or influence demand so strongly, so as to attain maximum advantage. **(Translator's Comment)**

that Marx had to assume the metaphysical personality of Aristotle in logical reasoning and analysis.

This is explicable, in that economic realities reflect phenomena that contradict the conclusions reached in Marxist theory. A conclusion arrived at through this theory is that capitalist profits vary from one firm to another, depending on the amount of work paid for during production processes, *irrespective* of the degree of mechanisation or level of utilisation of productive equipment, such as machines and tools.

The use of equipment does not add any extra value on production, according to Marx. Yet, we do notice in real life that high technology and automation do help generally in raising the level of profitability. It was, therefore, not possible for Marx to find practical economic circumstances supporting his assertion; he was forced instead to attempt an abstract proof. But as he fulfilled his task, the results fell much short of realistic economic life. In consequence, he resorted to the argument that the discrepancy resulted from perversions inherent in the capitalist system, which lead to deviations from the law of intrinsic value, due to the dominant role of the forces of supply and demand.

4.9 A CRITIQUE OF THE BASIS OF MARXIST ECONOMICS

It is now apt to examine the Marxist **theory of value**, in the light of the reasoning that was advanced for it. Marx begins - as noted earlier - by analysing the process of exchange, stressing that the essence of any product's value is the amount of labour embodied in it, irrespective of any other factor, such as the proper uses or characteristics of the item in question.

But what would be the Marxist view if we employed this method of analysis to look at the value of two products, one resulting from individual effort, the other from social production? If we look at a piece of ancient writing, and attempt to ascertain its market value, we may find that this is equal or approximate to, say, a copy of a history encyclopaedia.

In this instance, the ancient writing is a work of ***individual*** production - as Marxists would call it - while the encyclopaedia is an outcome of **social production**. How, then, could these two different items fetch a similar price? Could the mutual feature between them be the amount of labour expended on them? Of course not, because the time devoted to produce the ancient writing is very likely to have been much shorter than in the case of the encyclopaedia.

It is noteworthy that Marx had exempted ancient pieces and works of art from his theory of value, and it is not difficult to understand the reason for this exemption. Yet, in our example, there must be something common to the two items that makes their values similar, and we need to identify the mutual element to these two products, which are quite different in their features and the kind of utility bestowed upon their owner/user.

Is it not fair to say that this simple example illustrates that some common ingredient(s) must exist among products available in the market, other than the labour content embodied in each? And is it not possible to argue that such ingredient(s) need to be present in products characterised by individual effort, as well as those bearing the stamp of social production? And, if there was such a common thread - despite differences in labour content and type of labour effort, as well as product specifications and characteristics - why can it not be seen as the essence of value in exchange[10]?

It is plain from this that the analytic method used by Marx stalls half-way, and does not permit him to reach the requisite conclusions, as long as the labour content differs appreciably in cases where market

---

[10] In fact, economists have long established that a product/service must be recognised by consumers to render utility before they would be prepared to pay for it. This would be so, no matter what amount of labour content had been put into it. (**Translator's Comment**)

values of the respective products are similar. And, if labour content is not the underlying factor in determining value, what is?

There seems to be a major problem facing Marx's theory of value. This is the obvious clash between the theory and hard facts, which people notice and cope with in practice, whatever may be the prevailing political, cultural and ideological setting. Consequently, it is not possible for the theory to give a genuine and practical explanation of value.

If the land is taken as an example, we can see the clash between Marx's theory of value and practice. Farmland can be utilised for producing a variety of agricultural items, such as wheat, cotton, rice etc. As different plots of land vary in suitability for these items, it is clear that average and marginal productivity for any particular item will fluctuate among various areas.

This means in effect that the same amount of labour expended to produce wheat will result in a higher yield in the case of farmland appropriate for that item, than otherwise. Different similar-sized pieces of farmland grown with wheat for identical periods will give us differing quantities, each of which will fetch a particular market value. This value will hinge upon the quantity produced, and any differences in quality, if any.

Any farmer or a socialist country (or a non-socialist country for that matter) would be foolhardy to equate the value of two different lots of produce obtained form two areas of land, as such action would undervalue the output of more productive farms, overvalue that of the less productive, or both. It is therefore incumbent on any landowner, farming authority or a state apparatus, to attempt to put various areas of land to their best possible uses in accordance with their suitability, so as to enhance output and maximise gain.

It is also clear that differences in yield levels, procured from various pieces of farmland, may not be due to the amount of labour put into them, owing to the role played by the nature of land itself and the extent of its suitability for that type of produce[11]. We are thus back facing the same previous question: what is the true essence of any product/service that gives it value in exchange? While productive labour is significant in determining value, there must be other important elements that have to be spelled out.

Another phenomenon that Marxism has not been able to interpret, in the light of its theory of value, is the low market price, due to limited social interest in it. As tastes, fashions, and technology change, any given product may experience loss of market value.

Such changes may come about from developments in the spheres of politics, religion, ideology or other fields, resulting in diminished product value, despite the fact that the same content of social labour continues to be devoted in making the product. Once again, this illustrates that a product's utility in satisfying needs is highly instrumental in determining market value. It is thus a grave mistake to regard value in usage, along with the benefit actually derived from the product, as an insignificant variable.

Marxism ignores all this talk about the notion of consumer utility, preferring to replace it with the concept of 'supply and demand'. The Marxist focus remains, however, on social labour, as the true mirror of value of any product.

Yet, confusion and erroneous judgement may easily set in as a result. Marxists would readily concede that when productive conditions positively develop, the amount of social labour required would diminish, sending market value lower. Conversely, when production

---

[11] Marxists could concede these differences in land yield, and may opt instead to calculate an average yield for each type of item, so as to associate this with a given amount of labour. If one hour of labour is required to produce one kilogram of cotton in some farms, while on other farms two hours are needed, the average requisite amount of labour is 1.5 hours per kilogram, and therefore value would be affixed accordingly. Under these circumstances, Marxists would argue that an hour of labour on fertile land is equivalent to 1.5 hours of the social average, while an hour of work on infertile land equals 2/3 of the social average. But this reasoning begs the question, because how is it possible for an hour of work on fertile land to exceed itself? The extra half-hour is not the outcome of human effort, being the result of the higher quality of land.

parameters deteriorate, the labour needed would increase, and market value would rise as well.

Yet, this analysis focuses on the **supply** side, leaving aside the demand part of the equation. When production conditions in paper-manufacturing take a turn to the worse (e.g. lack of good quality materials or paucity of suitable equipment), the amount of labour needed to produce the same quantity of paper may double. Yet, if no increase in the quantity of labour was forthcoming, output would diminish, thereby sending the price up, due to a higher level of marginal utility.

The **reverse** might also be expected to occur. If production conditions improve (e.g. use of improved technology or newly-developed materials), requisite social labour would reduce. If the total amount of labour expended in paper making remained the same, production would increase substantially, and prices would fall, due to the abundance of paper and a reduction in its marginal utility.

It is clear, therefore, that changes in market price may coincide with changes in either the quantity available on the market or social labour required in production, or both. Such phenomena do not provide a conclusive proof that alterations in market value are necessarily the consequence of changes in social labour only; herein lies the confusion that may arise, and consequently the murkiness of the Marxist theory of value.

In addition, labour effort is *not* homogenous: it includes work elements that are diverse in nature, impact and significance. There is, on the one hand, artistic work which depends on special skills and experience, while there exists also other types of work that are unskilled and simple in nature. A working hour expended by a porter is vastly different from that of an architect; a day's work from a technical worker producing electric motors is bound to be far removed from that of a digger.

Personal factors represent another significant area affecting work and productivity, influencing - as they bound to do - the level of psychological and organic effort exerted by people. These factors shape the extent of the drive to work, as well as inner feelings and emotions, leading to certain attitudes that may be conductive, ambivalent, or even antagonistic towards work and productivity. Due to innate feelings and attitudes, a working person may possess an incentive or a disincentive to innovate; work may make him/her feel despondent and bored, or alternatively stimulated and hopeful.

It would therefore be a mistake to measure work in a purely quantitative manner; *qualitative* or descriptive criteria are required as well. An hour of work in congenial surroundings would be more productive, than otherwise. As it is necessary to measure the quantity of work, we also need to gauge its quality and characteristics, in the light of the various psychological parameters which impact upon it.

It is clear, therefore, that while we are able to measure the quantity of work through gauging output over time, it is more problematic to assess the quality, and the effect of relevant personal characteristics. Two *major* issues thus confront Marxism in this connection, these being:

A) How to measure the **quantity** of work, whether aesthetic or otherwise.

B) How to measure work **efficiency**, which is affected by psychological, organic and attitudinal variables.

In attempting to tackle the first issue, Marxists have suggested categorising work into two main types, simple and complex. *Simple* work is performed primarily through physical energy, without much need for cognitive capabilities. In contrast, *complex* tasks involve the use of expertise and accumulated knowledge, which are acquired over time (e.g. medical or engineering work).

Marxists regard basic (simple) tasks as the **yardstick** for measuring the value of work: complex tasks can be viewed as *multiples* of simple-work units. The value of a week's work-load for an electrical engineer, who designs electric motors, is much higher than a corresponding weekly load of a porter, due to the higher expertise of the engineer.

In essence, Marxists have suggested that the period devoted to training or education ought to *count* in assessing the value of complex (professional) work. An engineer who has ten years of experience behind him, plus twenty years of study, should be viewed as someone whose work is valued as equivalent to thirty years' experience. If we have a porter with a 15-year experience, then this person's work is valued at half the engineer's.

While all this may be acceptable to Marxists on paper, in practice economic life is very different. It is seldom the case, for instance, that an experienced electrical engineer works for double the wage of the porter, as usually he/she gets much more than that. And, the hard experience of socialist regimes (including the former Soviet Union) shows that pay differentials are glaringly wide: they are certainly larger than what is suggested by Marxist analysis. The definitive conclusion, therefore, is that pay levels must *reflect* the value of the work done by individuals, as judged and assessed by society at large, rather than determined arbitrarily through a simplistic or artificial criterion.

Concerning the second issue (i.e. measuring labour efficiency), the Marxist standpoint is summarised by taking a representative volume of social labour as the basis for calculating average value.

Accordingly, if a production operative possesses characteristics making him/her an above-average producer, then that individual's hourly output would exceed an average-worker's in a similar work setting. The error committed by Marxists in this regard is that they always study this problem from a quantitative angle only. Within the Marxist frame of thinking, a highly-skilled, or better-motivated operative, is simply one who produces at a higher rate than the average operative, setting aside important aspects, pertaining to such matters as quality improvements and technical innovation.

In practice, the extra cognitive, physical or psychological attributes displayed by the above-average worker are ***not*** always reflected in higher quantitative levels of productivity: they may be mirrored in higher product quality, creative changes in working methods or new ways in lowering costs or wastage levels[12]. In a similar fashion, one painter may produce an excellent portrait in one hour, while another's hourly output may be much less spectacular. Quite clearly, we are not dealing here merely with different quantitative levels of productivity. Even if we give the less skilled painter two hours, he/she may not provide an output similar to that of the better-able painter.

Plainly, therefore, the market value of the two paintings will differ, irrespective of political or other non-relevant factors, and it would be incorrect to insist that such variations in value are invariably due to the (equivalent) volume of individual or social labour embodied in the product. The gist of all this is that differences in value may result from **quality,** as well as the quantity, of labour.

These are some of the difficulties, which have obstructed the Marxist path, showing the insufficiency of the Marxist theory of value. Despite all this, however, Marx felt obliged to adhere to his theory, insisting that labour content is the essence of all value.

As indicated earlier, Marx missed an essential ingredient, in that he neglected the role of a product's **utility** to the consumer. This factor – which in modern economic theory provides the basis of demand analysis – may have such an impact as to equalise the market price of a wooden bed and a gentleman's suit (in a previously-mentioned

---

[12] What the learned author is saying here has its echo in the emphasis of modern management theory and practice on such important concepts as continuous improvement, employee empowerment, and Japanese-style quality circles. **(Translator's Comment)**

example), while in fact the labour content embodied in these two products may be quite different.

Consequently, the whole inference that Marx utilises to support his law of value comes ***crumbling down***. Other factors may, therefore, be just as important as labour, in explaining value – or indeed more so. Such factors may be psychological (e.g. prestige) or health-related in nature. It is only when we recognise the importance of consumer utility, and the factors which influence it, that we can overcome the problems faced by Marx's theory of value.

In the previous example concerning a piece of ancient writing and a history encyclopaedia, we may now be able to find the factor that lies behind their price parity. While the labour content of these two works may differ greatly, the social need for them may be nearer to equivalence. On this basis, also, other problematic elements in explaining value will dissolve as well.

As the need for any product or service emanates from the nature of the intended usage, this latter aspect can not be ignored in assessing value. Any product that has no value *in usage* can not have a value in exchange either – whatever labour effort is put in producing it. Marx admitted this, though he did not clarify the true nature of the link between value in usage and value in exchange.

While value in usage may be viewed as the main basis of consumer need, it is by no means the only factor in this regard. A general proportionate relationship can be envisaged between the use of any good and the wish to obtain it. Yet, scarcity is important here, in that a relatively scarce item will be attractive to many, while a plentiful item will not fetch a high market value. Air is an essential ingredient for human living, but it has no market value, owing to its natural availability in unlimited quantities.

4.10 MARXIST   CRITIQUE   OF   CAPITALIST SOCIETY

It may *appear* to some that spelling out Marxist criticisms of capitalism is intended to knock out these points, so as to support capitalist thinking, as the latter is recognised by Islamic principles.

Islam *permits* individual ownership of the means of production, and opposes the socialist system. Some have concluded form this that Islamists must endeavour to *discredit* Marxist claims regarding the capitalist system and capitalistic life-styles, giving convincing evidence to show the erroneous analysis of Marxists.

In fact, Islamic thinkers feel *no* obligation to defend capitalism and the realities of life under this system, including its social ramifications. What is required is to find the common ground between Islam an capitalism; Marxist analysis would need to be looked at, so as to clarify any relationship (positive or otherwise) with these mutual elements.

It would be wrong, therefore, for any principled Islamist to come to the defence of Western-style capitalism, denying all the evils and mistakes that are inherent in such a society. They may think that by doing so they are justifying the main tenets of Islamic economics, which accepts private ownership. But this line of thinking is *misguided*, and must be rejected.

It is equally wrong to approve the methods adopted by Marxists in analysing capitalism, so as to expose the destructive elements of the system. Marxism views **private ownership** as the prime source of all the negative aspects associated with the capitalist system throughout history. It is therefore in order here to emphasise two main points, so as to settle the Islamic stand towards Marxism and its assessment of capitalism:

First: it is not incumbent on principled Muslim researches to justify capitalism, or to attempt a correction of the various aspects of this system, denying the bitter realities that are associated with it.

Secondly: it would be a mistake to regard the historical facts of modern capitalism as presenting a true profile of any society permitting private ownership of the means of production. The conclusions derived from a study of capitalism *must not* be extended to other societies/systems that allow private ownership.

Marxists have condemned capitalism, due to the alleged consequences flowing from the private possession of property, and in keeping with their basic axiom in interpreting history, which maintains that the type of ownership in any society is the cornerstone in shaping the whole soco-economic structure. This, in effect, means that everything that takes place within a capitalist society have their roots in the economic sphere, especially private ownership of the means of production. These events/phenomena include social deprivation and misery; monopoly, business collusion and exploitation; armies of unemployed workforce; excesses of colonialism; contradictions within society.

In this connection, Islamic thinkers would submit that Marxists *confuse* two different issues, namely private ownership and the factual realities of capitalism. Capitalist societies have their own *special* ideological, political and economic features, resulting – as these do – in certain drawbacks, injustices and perversions. These latter consequences can not aptly be viewed as flowing directly form private ownership. Moreover, Marxism has erred in its alleged scientific analysis of the development of the capitalist system and its contradictions.

4.11 CONTRADICTIONS OF CAPITALISM

It is now possible to start looking at the chief **inconsistencies** within capitalism – as Marxists view them. The prime mover of these inconsistencies is **profit** generated through waged labour. Capitalists are alleged to earn vast profits via employing waged labourers, and this is seen as the prime source of contradiction within the whole system. Marx focused strongly on this aspect, attempting to unravel it in the course of developing his celebrated concept of **'added value'**.

In essence, Marx believed that any product's value is due primarily to the *amount of labour* expended on it. If an industrialist bought a £100-worth of wood, then employed a workman to produce a bed, to be sold at £200, the difference would be £100, which is shared by the labourer and the capitalist. If the industrialist pays £30 to the workman and keeps £70, then this latter figure is the *added value*. The worker is, therefore, required to produce value exceeding his own earning, so as to provide for the capitalist's profit.

It is a firm Marxist belief that this is the only explanation of the whole capitalist phenomenon. In effect, Marx refutes the contention that the entrepreneur/capitalist is **entitled** to compensation for putting up capital and devoting time and effort to run the business. For Marxists, the matter is quite simple, in that the value of any item must be equal to the total value of all the materials/components, machines/tools and labour expended in the course of production. What all this boils down to is that profit (or added value) is the element *pocketed* by the capitalist.

In Marxist thinking, labour occupies a *pivotal* role in determining the value of any item. Capitalists achieve profits through paying wage-earners much less than the true value of the work done – as measured by the difference between the product's market price and the total paid for all other inputs, such as materials and machines. Frequently, the capitalist pays the labourer only subsistence wages, that barely enable him/her to survive and renew his/her energies, while the added value is kept as 'profit'.

In expanding all this, Marx **believed** that he uncovered the prime contradiction afflicting the capitalist system, in that the owner/capitalist purchases from wage-earners their **labour**, while these workers actually **create** the value of the relevant item. The worker is only paid for part of his/her effort, while the remainder is *stolen* by the capitalist as a 'surplus'. All this furnishes fertile ground for the class struggle, between the proletariat and the capitalist class.

Clearly, the theory of added value views labour as the prime source of any product's value. If the workman receives all the value that he/she created, nothing will be left to others. Hence, for something to be left over to the owner/capitalist, the latter must siphon off a portion from what the operative/worker have created. The Marxist theory of added value is thus based on the 'law of value', as Marxists what call it, and the two are inextricably liked. If the Marxist law of value is proved to have failed, the theory of added value collapses too; so will all other theories of Marxist economics, which depend on that so-called law.

As has already been illustrated above, labour content is **not** necessarily the prime essence of value in exchange. Frequently, **social need** (i.e. utility) is viewed as the real determinant of value in exchange, and therefore it is not necessarily correct to *interpret* profit as part of the value created by workers – as Marx did. Furthermore, we cannot ignore the role of materials/components, which have relative scarcity, in giving value to products. Wood, for example, does have value in exchange, and therefore contributes towards bestowing value on the wooden bed, in the light of the importance of social need. This is despite the fact that virtually no human labour is expended in making the wood itself. The same is true of other natural materials that are embodied in producing various goods. Marxism ignored the role of materials, claiming instead that these have no value in exchange, as long as there is no labour expended in making them available.

It is true that raw materials appear to possess little value while they remain below the surface of Earth, or even above. But when labour is applied to these materials, the latter's value is enhanced. However, this hardly means that raw materials have no value in exchange, and that any value they have is the consequence of the labour content combined with them.

Labour utilised in mining important metals (e.g. gold) results in the provision of items that are highly valued by the market. Conversely, when the same labour is exerted on extracting low-value materials (e.g. ordinary rocks), the materials obtained may be almost worthless. Hence, the two elements (i.e. material and labour) are integrated and interlocked in producing a worthwhile value that can be exchanged, e.g. precious metals, diamonds, or crude oil. Each has its specific part in evolving the final value that is recognisable in the marketplace.

Apart from labour and materials, other inputs must be given their proper recognition in determining the value of final products. In the case of farm output, for instance, the fertility of land is highly instrumental in attaining value. In the case of manufacturing, major contributions to the production process are provided by inputs such as energy, machines and tools.

The upshot of all this is that the final value of any product is shaped and determined ***not simply by labour effort***, but also by other inputs. Hence, the worker is not the only source of value for any given product; consequently any 'added value' - if any - need not by part of the value created by labour, as it can equally result from contributions by other inputs such as materials, energy and land.

When a product's value is drawn - either partly or largely - from natural factors (e.g. raw materials), a question arises concerning the party to whom any added value duly belongs. Should it belong to the worker(s), or to somebody or something else? This point is beyond the area dealt with here, as the focus of this debate is on the link between labour and added value, and whether the latter is part of the former.

When Marx presented his thesis that labour was the only source of value, he could not explain the notion of added value (profit) except through ***assuming*** that it was an ingredient created by labour effort. As has now been clarified, it is perfectly possible to understand added value as something that can be brought about by non-labour inputs. As society progresses, new ways of merging labour with materials are developed, whereby novel products or designs are invented, which will have market values based on the inputs embedded in them. The values of these new products will be over and above the total sum of the values assumed separately by each input.

There is something else that Marxists did not take into consideration, namely the value created by the entrepreneur/founder of any project/business. Such a value results from the innovative and managerial abilities of these individuals, who make the whole endeavour possible, including the day-to-day running of the enterprise itself. It has been established, through hard facts and ample evidence, that projects starting with equal sums of capital, as well as similar other features and inputs including workforce, may end up with very different outcomes in terms of performance and profits, owing to differences in the capabilities and aptitudes of top management.

It has thus been well documented that management is a pivotal element in the whole process of production, and the degree of success that can be accomplished. It is not sufficient simply to gather workers, tools, machines and materials: the project would require a leader who could make the wheel turn, through taking appropriate decisions, including the recruitment of the requisite labour force, selecting types and qualities of materials and so on.

Quite apart from setting up the whole project, duties of each individual employee must be defined, work has to be monitored, and goods/services produced must be marketed. If labour is the essence of value, then it is imperative to take note of the leadership and managerial work performed by any entrepreneur/manager. Accordingly, it is **impossible** for Marx to find any basis for his theory of added value, except in cases where the capitalist acquires profit *without* putting any effort in entrepreneurship or management.

And, when the Marxist theory of added value is found wanting, then the concept of **class struggle** crumbles. This latter concept is derived from the alleged existence of major contradictions within the capitalist system. A major such contradiction is between worker and owner, whereby the latter is supposed to steal or siphon off some of the value created by the labourer. Another contradiction is between what the owner purchases from the worker as his/her labour-energy, while what is actually received by the capitalist is labour *itself* which is more valuable.

As has now been argued, profit **need not** result from value created by labour, and hence it is by no means certain that the capitalist is stealing from his employees some of their labour. This demolishes the very basis of class struggle between the capitalist class and so-called *proletariat*.

No one doubts that there is some **clash** of interest between worker and capitalist, as far as the distribution of the gross-revenue cake is concerned. Workers are keen to have higher pay and better working conditions, while owners would suffer lower profits when they capitulate to these demands. But this is quite different from the Marxist notion of class struggle, which views contradiction and blackmail as an integral component of the capital-worker relationship. Clashes of interest occur in the ordinary course of dealings between producer and customer, for example.

Regarding the contradiction between what the owner purchases from the worker and what the latter actually delivers, this really depends on the above-mentioned Marxist claim that owners contract to obtain the worker's energy not the labour *per se*, while actually exacting the latter. In Marx's view, labour is the essence of value, and the fundamental yardstick by which any product's value is measured. In contrast, the work-energy expresses an amount of effort expended - or the necessary subsistence of the worker - and therefore is something that can have a given value and bought by the capitalist.

In Islamic economics, the owner does **not own** the worker's labour, **nor** does he/she buy the worker's energy. Neither labour nor labour energy is the product that is bought by the owner; the latter only purchases the **benefit** of the wage-earner's labour, i.e. the materialistic outcome flowing from the worker's interface with natural materials/equipment.

A man who possesses wood along with associated equipment may hire a workman to produce a wooden bed, paying him a fee/wage for performing the requisite work. The wooden bed, which is produced through labour effort, is the resultant benefit of the labour expended by the workman; this labour is purchased and paid for by the owner of the business. In effect, therefore, it is this **labour benefit** that is purchased by the owner, and must be clearly differentiated from labour *per se*, or even labour energy. This labour benefit is also not an integral part of a person's entity: it is essentially a good having a given value commensurate to the nature of benefit rendered. The owner procures from workers the benefit of their labour, and receives this benefit in the form of wood that becomes a wooden bed, without any inconsistency between what is *contractually bought* and what is *actually obtained* by the owner.

It is pertinent to note the difference between labour benefit, on the one hand, and relatively scarce natural materials, such as wood and minerals. While all these have value in exchange, labour benefit possesses a **special characteristic**, in that it is endowed with the element of human will and possibility of choice. Through human action, work can be made *more* scarce and its value raised, as frequently resorted to by labour unions and professional bodies, which embark upon various types of industrial action such as strikes. It may thus seem - on the surface - that the value of labour is determined arbitrarily, depending on the will and strength of organised labour. Yet, the fact remains that the value of labour is determined through the same general mechanism as other goods, though human will may occasionally intervene in this process[13].

---

[13] In fact, this human intervention, referred to by the author, does also occur in the case of non-labour items, such as materials or equipment. Group action/understanding/collusion among traders or producers have been known to impact on market values of relevant items. **(Translator's Comment)**

Having studied the Marxist notion of added value, it is now possible to look at other phases of Marx's analysis of capitalist society. After expounding his two fundamental concepts of **general value** and **added value**, which led him to the conviction that capitalism contained major contradictions, he proceeded to infer certain so-called 'laws' that would result inevitably in the demise of that system.

A prime such law was the **class struggle** , in which wage-earners indulge against the capitalist class, due to the latter's theft of part of the value created by the former. Then comes another 'law' which intensifies the struggle, namely the law of falling profits, or the general trend of business profits to diminish.

The whole idea of this so-called 'law' is based on the belief that **competition** among businesses will force capitalists to devote a portion of their profits for product/technological development and marketing efforts. An intensive race is bound to occur, whereby each owner will attempt not only to hold his/her ground, but also to improve products/designs/technologies, and to enter new markets, in order to withstand the onslaught of competitors or surpass them. All this will make inroads into business profits, necessitating the need to accumulate large business capital to ensure survival, and the reduction of average returns on investment.

Marx was well aware of the phenomenon of scientific and technological progress, and reckoned that it would lead to ***increasing*** automation of industrial operations, thereby lowering average labour usage. As labour content is curtailed - Marx argued - the scope for profit-making would fall back as well, leading to another crisis at the very heart of the capitalist system.

Such a scenario would prompt capitalists to press workers to ***cut*** wages, so as to preserve the amount of added value (profit), Marx thought. Alternatively, workers would be hard pressed to work more for the same wages. Either way, the conflict between the two sides would intensify, and the miserable conditions of the working class would deteriorate further.

Marx was also clear in identifying the adverse **multiplier** effects which follow *en masse* income reduction for society in general. He believed that any lowering in pay-levels for working people would diminish purchasing power in the hands of individuals and families, resulting inevitably in shrinking demand levels for goods and services in the general economy. Capitalists would thus have to search for new markets, most likely abroad, thus embarking on the colonialist - and monopolistic - era of capitalism, in order to secure the continued luxurious life-style of the ruling elite.

Marx contended that such developments would *sharpen* the class struggle, whereby the weaker members of the bourgeoisie class would fall by the wayside, whereby the proletariat class would be *expanded*, and society becomes polarised even further. Simultaneously, the bourgeoisie class would lose their colonies, as a consequence of the march of liberation movements among colonised regions, which would create yet more problems and hardship for members of the capitalist class. Ultimately, the historic curve must reach a decisive juncture, at which the whole capitalist edifice would come crumbling down, as a product of revolutionary turmoil that is ignited wittingly be workers and other members of the oppressed class.

The above concepts and arguments profile a summary of the analytic phases of capitalism, as envisaged by Marxism. Several points can be put forward in this connection:

First: the so-called law of class struggle is based on the potential contradiction evoked by profit, and hinges on the correctness of the theory of added value. When the latter theory collapses - as has already been demonstrated - the alleged contradiction will vanish, and the whole concept of class struggle becomes shaky, to say the least.

Second: regarding the claim of diminishing profits, Marxist analysis here is based on its central assertion concerning value (the so-called **law of value**). Marx noted that falling labour content would reduce the potential for profit-making, as profit was part of the value created by labour effort. As it has now been well established, labour is not the only source of value, and it is perfectly possible for reduced labour content, coupled with increased automation and more use of modern equipment, to leave business profit undiminished - or even raise it to a higher level.

Third: there is the presumed increasing phenomenon of misery among working classes. This so-called law is viewed to be the consequence of higher levels of unemployment, which come about from replacing labour with machines. In Marx's words, this leads to a 'reserve army of the unemployed' for the benefit of capitalists, as a direct consequence of continual technological progress. The inevitable product of all this is widespread misery and poverty; even starvation here and there.

In fact, this so-called 'law' was taken up by Marx from **Ricardo's analysis** of the effects of mechanisation on workers life, and how such a process would create and enlarge unemployment in society. However, Marx added another element, namely the *replacement* of skilled labour by unskilled operatives, who would work for less, due to work simplification resulting from enhanced automation. All this would limit the bargaining power of labour, and lead to heightened misery almost by the day.

Marxists, however, faced a **dilemma** when they discovered that miserable conditions were far from being a fact of life for the working masses in the capitalist West, in the USA and Western Europe. Their response was that 'misery' was a comparative phenomenon, in that the gap between rich and poor was widening, despite the general improvement in the life-styles of the working class - in the absolute sense. Yet, this does not legitimise their claim that social misery was spreading, and that this would result in an explosion that would wreck the whole structure of capitalism.

Fourth: it is in order to enquire about the true factors behind want, destitution and misery, which Marx viewed as ever present in a capitalist system. In truth, such negative phenomena were *not* the consequence of private ownership, but essentially due to the *capitalist pattern* of that ownership. In its classical form, capitalism did not recognise the principle of public ownership, and gave private owners free reign to possess all means of production, as well as to indulge in various types of activities. In addition, the original form of the capitalist system contained no provision for social security, in cases of unemployment, sickness and old age. Nor were there adequate constraints on how owners should use their possession of the means of production, so as not to cause detriment to the overall interest of society.

A totally new situation would come about when private ownership is permitted in principle; at the same time some means of production and certain activities were devoted to public ownership, while a wide-ranging social security system is instituted. In effect, there would be a carefully mixed economy, with economic freedoms being limited within the confines of what is considered to be in the general good, so that ownership is not allowed to become concentrated in the hands of the few, and cases of gross abuse would be prevented. A society which adopts such an economic strategy should not display much misery, need or destitution that have been known to raise their ugly heads within a system of unfettered capitalism.

Lastly: Marxism looks at colonialism as a purely economic phenomenon, regarding it as a necessary product of the advanced stages of capitalism, due to the insufficiency of domestic markets. In fact, colonialism is **not** an accompaniment of the later capitalist phases, but well and truly a practical reflection of the materialistic frame of mind. Colonialism is an eloquent expression of the materialistic mind-set, in all its associated demeanour, notions about life, and practical objectives. It is all these that make the seeking of **maximum** profit the overriding aim, irrespective of the means employed, moral dimensions or long-term consequences.

The testimony to all this is available from hard facts, because the beginnings of colonialism can be traced to the early stages of capitalism in European societies, with its general framework of thinking and criteria. By the time capitalism advanced to the higher stages, colonialism became an economic necessity, and European powers had divided the regions of the weaker nations among themselves in an audacious and highly aggressive manner.

Britain laid hands on India, Burma, South Africa, Egypt, Sudan, and many other nations. To France, belonged Indo-China, Algeria, Morocco, Tunisia, Madagascar and other colonies. Germany had areas in West Africa and the Pacific Rim; Italy had Somalia and Tripoli; Belgium colonised Congo; Russia obtained sectors in Asia.

The original and realistic motive behind colonialism can be found in the spiritual field and the type of social demeanour within the respective nations. In itself, the existence of private property does not fully explain colonialism. When private ownership is allowed within a society endowed with strong and righteous spiritual, behavioural and political frameworks, colonialism is **not** a necessary and inevitable by-product.

Nor is **monopoly** a forgone conclusion in a society allowing private ownership of the means of production. Monopoly can be viewed as the consequence of unlimited liberty granted to owners of the means of production. It results essentially from the system of *laisser faire*, which preclude the State from intervening in the economic life of the nation. But when the proper checks and balances are in place, with a sufficient role to the State, monopolistic practices and domination by the few are never going to be the inevitable result of private ownership.

~ *Chapter Five* ~

Socialism and Communism

It was pointed out from the outset in this book that an **economic doctrine** was tantamount to a general framework for living, the proponents of which demand its application, so as to manage social existence on its basis, regarding it as the best strategy available to attain for humanity the prime objectives of decent living and happiness. As for the nature of **economic sciences**, these are studies which set the basis through which humans develop frameworks to govern society in the economic sphere.

A doctrine, therefore, is a general design for action, as well as a call to follow a given path. A science, on the other hand, aims to uncover the truth and any hidden laws of nature. For this reason, doctrines have an active role in the overall process of renewal and innovation, while science is pre-occupied mainly with recording what happens in a systematic and objective fashion without interference, re-moulding, or exercising much discretion on the part of the scientist.

On this basis, previous chapters of this book *distinguished* between historical materialism and the Marxist doctrine. The first (i.e. historical materialism) pertains to the development and growth of production, along with associated consequences in the economic, political and ideological fields. In other words, it is the science of Marxist economics, which interprets the whole of history from an economic angle, in the light of the nature and progress sustained by the production forces.

In contrast, Marxist doctrine is a socio-economic system that had been put forward by Marxists, calling upon all people in various parts of the globe to strive towards its implementation. In a way, the stance of Marxist leaders vis-à-vis historical materialism is similar to that of the natural scientist in relation to the laws of nature. Wearing their doctrinal hat, Marxists assume a missionary posture, attempting to convince all others that heir cause is fair, practical and inevitable.

Despite this contrast between science and doctrine, there is a strong bond between the two. The doctrine advocated by Marxists is essentially an expression and a recipe for a specific phase within the various stages of historical materialism. It is nothing but a segment of the general historical curve that reflects – in Marxist thinking – the thrust and momentum of production, along with relevant laws and contradictions. Marxists, therefore, look upon their doctrinal call as a simple truth embodied in historical laws: it implements the will of history and echoes the requirements of the economic factor, which beckons the human bandwagon towards the new stage, that which embodies the whole strategy of the Marxist doctrine.

For this reason, Marx labelled his doctrine as **'scientific socialism'**, to distinguish it from other types of socialism, where others had striven to express their own proposals, wishes or feelings. In these variant forms of 'socialism', non-Marxists have not necessarily expressed a historical inevitability, associated with pertinent 'laws', and hence they formulated their respective doctrines at a distance from scientific accounts; without ample study of the productive forces and their development.

According to Marxist doctrine, there are two prime stages which need to be put in practice, namely **socialism** and **communism**. Marxists stress that both of these stages are inevitable, and they are dictated by the sheer scientific movement of history. Based on the theory of historical materialism, **communism** is the uppermost stage of human development, because in it the greatest miracle will be accomplished, and the forces of production will have the absolute upper hand.

Socialism, on the other hand, will be built on the rubbles of capitalism, and will directly and effectively replace the latter. In one sense, socialism is a repercussion of the inevitable and an historic revolt against capitalism, when the latter enters its final decadent period. In another sense, socialism is a necessary condition to prepare humanity for communist society, guiding therefore the human voyage to the right shores.

5.1 CHARACTERISTICS OF SOCIALISM AND COMMUNISM

Each of these two distinct and historical phases (i.e. socialism and communism), possesses certain special features, which distinguish it from the other. The *characteristics* of the socialist stage may be summed under four chief points:

First: eradication of the class system, and its final liquidation with the setting up of a classless society.

Second: assumption by the proletariat of the political apparatus, whereby a totalitarian regime is established, with ample capability to implement the historic message of socialism.

Third: nationalisation of sources of wealth and means of production within the country. Such wealth and means will be owned by all, instead of being utilised by private owners through waged labour.

Fourth: distribution of wealth and income will be guided by the principle: *every person contributes their labour, and each will receive according to work implemented.*

When the human trail reaches the summit of the historical pyramid, i.e. true communism, change and development will be drastic and omnipresent. Communism will preserve the *first* cornerstone of socialism, namely erasing the class system, while other elements will be open for re-moulding and re-shaping.

As regards socialism's *second* cornerstone (rule of the proletariat), communism puts an end to the phenomenon of government and politics on the historical theatre, as the government of the proletariat will exist no longer, and society will be rid of the need for government and the constraints it imposes. The nationalisation of capitalist means of production (socialism's third cornerstone) will be taken a huge stage further, when the idea of individual ownership of those means (where no waged labour is employed) will be ironed out as well.

In addition, private ownership of consumer goods will be ruled out, thereby imposing a blanket ban on all private ownership in fields of production and consumption alike. Important adjustments will take place on socialism's fourth cornerstone, which pertains to distribution. The new slogan under communism is that all will *give according to their abilities, and receive according to their needs*.

This in a nutshell is the Marxist doctrine, in both its stages, socialism and communism. Any doctrine can be critically analysed by employing three different methodologies, these being:

A) critique of the main principles and ideological bases on which the doctrine is based.

B) studying the extent to which those principles/bases actually furnish the logical grounding for the doctrine.

C) researching the essential concept of the doctrine, with regard to possibilities of application, i.e. whether the concept is realistic or unrealistic in actual practice.

5.2   OVERALL CRITIQUE OF THE DOCTRINE

Right from the outset, a most fundamental question arises regarding the evidence on which the Marxist doctrine is based. Such evidence - if it could it made available - would form the required underpinning for the Marxist call, as well as the rationale for its implementation and structuring human life accordingly.

It must be said that Marx did **not** rely on any moral or egalitarian notions in developing or supporting his theory or reasoning, rather unlike many other socialists whom Marx would describe as 'idealistic' or 'imaginary'. In Marx's view, all value judgements are nothing but a product of economic circumstances and the social environment surrounding the productive forces. Consequently, there is no point in propagating a social set-up on purely moral grounds.

Instead, Marx would rely on the so-called laws of historical materialism, which explain the march of history, in accord with changes and developments in the state of the productive forces. He regarded those laws as the bedrock for any scientific explanation of history, viewing them as the power which generates change along the sequence of phases, depending on the shape and detailed position of the productive forces. As a result, he concluded that socialism was an **inevitable** outcome of those 'laws'. Their functioning lead to the surfacing of serious contradictions within capital societies, with the effect of destroying the system, thus paving the path for the building of socialism.

In debating the theory of historical materialism, this book has reached some non-Marxist conclusions. It has become clear that the historical bandwagon of humanity does **not** travel in the fashion dictated by historic materialism. Nor does human history necessarily derive its social essence from the state of the productive forces, their contradictions and so-called 'laws'. Over previous pages of this work, it has been shown that Marxism had erred in the very analysis it employed to expose the alleged inconsistencies of capitalism, and the supposed movement of the latter towards its forgone demise. All those inconsistencies took for granted the Marxist laws of 'value' and 'added value'. As these two pillars were demolished, the whole structure came crumbling down.

Even if we suppose that Marxists are correct in their analysis of the capitalist economy and the supposed perish of the latter owing to its inherent and deep-rooted problems, it does not automatically follow that capitalism would be replaced by socialism. The fall of capitalism, particularly in its classical form, would render the path wide open to several alternatives, such as the mixed State-private economy. Marxist socialism is only one possibility.

Consequently, Marxism would lose its scientific rigour, and become devoid of historic necessity, that is assumed to be derived from the laws of historic materialism. When the scientific cloak is removed, Marxism assumes a suggestive posture, similar to that of any other doctrine proposed on the table.

5.3   SOCIALISM

It is now time to look in some detail at the various **facets** of socialism. A prime feature of this system is *erasing* social classes, supposedly ending the various forms of struggle that have been a hallmark of human history throughout all times. All those struggles can be traced to class conflict, which has been the accompanying product of the *division* of society into 'haves' and 'have-nots'. When socialism is established, there will only be one social class, and thus class struggle will vanish, thereby terminating all types of social friction and the ground will be set firmly for harmony and peace for ever.

All this is based on the central idea of historical materialism, which maintains that the economic factor is the pivotal consideration in the life of any society. This very concept had led Marxism to the conclusion that the institution of **private ownership** had resulted in the division of the human race into 'haves' and 'have-nots', providing thus the whole basis of class structure in any society. As private ownership would be abolished under socialism, the whole rationale of class conflict would melt away, and it becomes impossible for class structure to continue in existence.

However, previous chapters of this work have looked at the theory of historic materialism, and it has been established that the economic factor (including the institution of private ownership) is **not** the sole consideration shaping history and historical events throughout the ages. As has previously been noted, social-class structures are **known** to been built on military, political or religious foundations. It is therefore not essential for the class system to wither away, as a consequence of the eradication of private ownership. In any society, other bases may be adopted for the formation of social class, and this applies to a socialist system as any other.

Indeed, when we analyse the socialist phase, we do find that it leads - by virtue of its economic and political nature - to the creation of a **new** category of class conflict. If we look at the economic nature of socialism (from each according his/her ability, and to each according to his/her contribution), a new type of disparity would inevitably come about. But more about this will be said later. Now, let us consider the political state of the socialist era.

The essential condition for the accomplishment of the revolutionary socialist experience is that it is implemented at the hands of skilful revolutionaries, who undertake the leadership role. It is not reasonable for every member of the proletariat to participate in leading and directing the experience; these many individuals must act in accord with directions of a competent leadership. For this reason, Lenin emphasised in the aftermath of the revolt of 1905 that it was incumbent on expert revolutionaries alone to form a new party, of the Bolshevik pattern.

In consequence, we found that the revolutionary leadership of the working class was a natural position for those calling themselves 'expert revolutionaries'. In a similar fashion, the leaders of previous revolutionary movements effected by peasants and workers were not necessarily workers or farmers themselves. However, a basic difference can be detected between the two situations, in that during socialism, the differentiating characteristic of leaders is not dominant economic circumstance, but -instead- ideological, revolutionary and party-related qualities.

All this is very interesting, when we inspect actual 20th century experience of socialist regimes in Eastern Europe. The revolutionary-cum-party cloak was a cover over the true nature of the socialist experience perpetrated on those nations. People could not - at the beginning - ascertain the true colours of the individuals who assumed leadership roles in those socialist experiments, which spawned the seeds for what Marxism would regard as the worst types of class-related differences in history. The underlying factor that had given such unrivalled power to those individuals was the Marxist view that the ruling body during socialism needed to possess *absolute* authority and total dominance, so as to settle all scores with capitalism in a decisive manner.

It is therefore clear that a marked feature of the socialist stage is the requirement for top leaders to continue the revolutionary programme and totalitarian mode of government, both within the party and state. The aim of all this is alleged to be the creation of the new socialist individual, who is completely devoid of all ills associated with class-dominated societies and exploitive tendencies that humanity endured over thousands of years.

What we actually find in practice is that when these 'socialist' leaders *reach* the reins of power, they (along with their entourage) come to possess vast capabilities, the likes of which had not been enjoyed by any privileged class throughout history. Socialist leaders become a class of their own, with unlimited authority over all assets and nationalised means of production in the land. They come to enjoy a political status, which enable them to take advantage of those assets/means, and utilise them for their own private interest - all with a firm belief that their dominance would secure happiness and prosperity to all individuals, precisely as other advantaged cliques thought over the feudalist and capitalist eras.

Virtually, the only difference is that erstwhile ruling cliques existed and developed - in the Marxist view - because of property/ownership relationships among people. The nature of those relationships determined whether any given person would be classified under one class or another. Under socialism, a different criterion would be in place, as the people who enjoy special privileges are those who possess power and happen to be in government.

The explanation of this class phenomenon under socialism, as distinct from other class-based systems, is clear. The dominant group/class in socialist societies did not grow and develop because of the economic factor, which was decisive in other systems - as Marxists would have us believe. In contrast, the group which takes charge of the state under socialism grows and develops on the political level, within a framework that has its special features. In effect, this framework is the **party mechanism**, which has its particular ideological and doctrinal features. The revolutionary party has its own philosophical basis; it leads the experiment; it is the training ground for the ruling class.

In the light of these class-related conditions, it is possible to understand the types of contradictions and political strife that frequently engulf socialist countries, as these often exhibit themselves in sweeping 'purges' or 'cleansing' operations. It is impossible for the group wielding effective power to include all party members, and members of the dominant group would inevitably have their private or special connections outside the party hierarchy.

The ruling elite may very well face some opposition within the party apparatus, especially from those members excluded from the echelons of genuine decision-making. In some cases, certain members may have been sacked by the leadership, and would naturally subscribe to the standpoint that the novel class system that developed betrays the fundamental principles of Marxism. In addition, the party leadership may encounter criticisms from outside the party, mainly from those alienated by the activities and extended links of official organs and state officials. As a result, it is only to be expected that wide-ranging **purges** - as communists would label them - would take place, as a reflection of those conditions and class-related conflicts. It would be natural for these events to be extensive and harsh, owing to the pervasive power possessed by the ruling elite in the State and party.

The fact that such phenomena impact on the top brass of the party, as well as the grassroots, indicates the seriousness and comprehensiveness of such events. Their frequency and violent nature may well exceed anything that Marxists have referred to as forms of class conflict over past historic epochs. In one situation back in 1936, a purge swept from power nine ministers in the former Soviet Union (out of an eleven-strong cabinet), in addition to top officials within the State and party machines, including many high-ranking officers in the armed forces. In another case in 1939, some two million Soviet communist members were expelled, out to a 2.5 million strong membership.

The aim of detailing such accounts here is not to smear the ruling apparatus within a socialist setting. Libels and smears have no place in this book. What is aimed at is a scientific analysis of socialism, so as to show that the system's materialistic and dictatorial essence is bound to result in class-related conditions that spawn repugnant kinds of conflict. The experiment which was supposed to eradicate class differences would thus develop a new type of class stratum.

If we now turn to the second main pillar of socialism, namely the **dictatorship of the proletariat,** we find that it is required not merely for settling scores with capitalism. As a temporary necessity - according to Marxist thinking - this dictatorship is needed to erase all traces of capitalism, whether spiritual, ideological or social. But, more than that, such at totalitarian framework mirrors deeply the true nature of Marxist socialism, which adheres passionately to the axiom of **central economic planning** in all spheres of activity and economic life.

The institution of such a planning system requires strong central authority, which has at its disposal ample and wide-ranging resources - free from detailed monitoring by others. Such a profile would enable the central planning organisation to *dictate* what, how and when various activities must be implemented in all fields and areas, on the basis of a master and fairly detailed blueprint. By its nature, central planing imposes on the political leadership a totalitarian colour.

Then we come to the third cornerstone of socialism, i.e. **nationalisation**. The prime scientific rationale for this rests on the alleged contradictions caused by the Marxist notion of 'added value'. In Marxist analysis, 'added value' has a particular meaning - as illustrated in previous chapters - and it results directly from the institution of private property. The consequential contradictions flowing from added value make it an imperative, as well as an historic necessity, that all means of production will be nationalised.

Previous pages of this book have dealt with these supposed contradictions, showing how they hinge on erroneous analysis. It is only to be expected that wrong conclusions would follow form misguided and mistaken foundations.

As for the *doctrinal concept* of 'nationalisation', this can be summed up thus: ending of private ownership would endow the whole society with holding the means of production in the land, so that each individual would become an owner of general or common wealth, on par with everybody else. In practice, however, this concept would clash with the prevailing political set-up during socialism, where the governing elite would enjoy virtually unchallenged privileges, in both party and State.

It is, therefore, not enough to put a legal end to private ownership of the means of production, declaring henceforth that ownership will revert to all, so that each and every individual would bask in the benefits that this will bring, and thus find the real essence of this new state of affairs in their own life-styles. The hard facts are such that the nitty-gritty of the political system will make it very likely that the ordinary individual's stake in national wealth is no more than nominal. The ruling class will taste the crux of this wealth, due to their blanket control of the nation's endowments and capabilities.

In consequence, the ruling elite under socialism will enjoy the same opportunities and benefits as monopolistic capitalists within a capitalist system. In fact, a case can be made out for the assertion that the socialist ruling class will be better placed than any capitalist to appropriate additional value and utilise national wealth for private advantage. This is because this class will stand at the summit of the whole system, vetting and/or engendering all major initiatives by the State or party, assuming the role of representing the class-less society and disposing of commonly-owned assets. What are the guarantees, therefore, to prevent abuse of power and misappropriation of national wealth for private gain?

To use Marxist terminology, it is possible to claim that nationalisation under Marxist socialism will raise the spectre of a conflict between socialist ownership for the general good - on the one hand - and the practical essence of ownership where benefits flow well and truly to the dominant class. In reality, the *gist* of ownership is **power over wealth**, and ability to reap advantage from it in various ways. This in effect is what the political forces can enjoy, owing to their total domination of all facets of society, as reflected on the constitutional and legal fronts, under the guise of privileges and rights.

These privileges and rights, as well as associated duties and authorities, are nothing but a fake cloak, interpreting - as they do - the essence of realistic ownership. A fundamental feature that distinguishes these new owners within Marxist socialism is that they cannot legally declare their ownership, due to the potential and direct clash with their political status. Because of the essential nature of socialism, the seeds of this type of owners are sown, despite the fact that prevailing *realpolitik* requires total denial of such a role/description. The political-cum-economic system is such that the new leaders are more coy about admitting such ownership, than their capitalist predecessors, many of whom would happily boast of their private possessions quite openly.

Nor is nationalisation under Marxist socialism an historically unique or unparalleled phenomenon. History contains past experiments in this field. In a number of regions, means of production had been nationalised, where outcomes resembled very broadly those under Marxist socialism. In certain past Hellenistic fiefdoms (especially in ancient Egypt), the State apparatus had adopted a strategy of nationalisation, where direct official control over most branches of production and distribution was exercised, resulting thereby in substantial benefits to the State. However, when public ownership came to be applied within the context of absolute rule exhibited by the Pharaonic mould, the realistic essence of the system could not be disguised.

It is clear, therefore, that when nationalisation takes place against a background of a totalitarian set-up, collective ownership will lead effectively to the domination of the governing elite over State-held assets, and the virtual conduct of those assets in a manner that serves the interests of the group which happens to be in power. Thus, we find that treachery and embezzlement by public officials is as old as public ownership itself, in addition to the surfacing of absolute rule on the part of the king/ruler, so much so that the latter soon assumes the title of a 'god' whereby huge resources would be expended to provide luxuries and pleasures for this person, in the form of palaces, places of worship, grave-shrines and such likes.

In view of all this, it is not surprising that nationalisation in ancient Pharaonic times was associated with similar facets to those exhibited by Marxist nationalisation in the modern epoch. Some may see important advantages in this system, especially in expanding production. Other aspects are negative, such as creeping State intervention, and *de facto* domination of a restricted clique over all

nationalised assets.   Under both the Pharaonic and Marxist
experiments, nationalisation led to the expansion of output in the
early stages, due to initial enthusiasm, but a dominant class soon
came into being, which recognised no limits to its authority, arguing
in the process that social growth and economic development
necessitated an iron hand.

Under both regimes, therefore, authoritarian rule became glaringly
apparent. Those who were in power tasted the essential attributes of
ownership, since nationalisation was not based on any spiritual
fundamentals or moral convictions.   Instead, materialism provided
the real basis, so much so that the strive to accomplish more output,
as well as surrounding rulers with the trappings of power, were
normal pursuits and consequences. It was also natural that the top
brass would not acquiesce to the practical meaning of public
ownership, except in so far as this would be an incentive for
increasing production.

It is not surprising, therefore, that the State apparatus - both old and
new - would be rampant with corruption and deceit on the part of
officials, who enriched themselves at the expense of public interest.
An example from the latter (Soviet-era) experience was where Stalin
found it necessary to admit that prominent State officials had
exploited their position, while there was pre-occupation with the
running of the second world war, resulting in the amassing of huge
wealth for those individuals.

All that indicates how far the two socialist experiments have been
similar, in both phenomena and outcome, despite differences in the
shape of civil society and production patterns. We also know from
this the nature of the consequences resulting from any nationalisation
experiment, if it is within the political framework of Marxism, which
calls for absolute authority, allegedly justified by the need to develop
production, which is viewed as the dominant momentum throughout
all times - within the context of historical materialism.

The last major cornerstone of socialism ,i.e. each giving according to capability and receiving according to contribution, is based, from the practical standpoint, on the laws of historical materialism. As we are led to believe that under modern socialism, there is only one class, it becomes incumbent on every person of working age to have a job, in order to live. The Marxist law which says that *labour* is the explanation of all value makes it inevitable that every individual capable of working must have a job, and receive commensurate compensation. Hence, the axiom that *from each according to ability, and to each according to contribution*.

However, in practice this principle may *contradict* the notion that society is made up of only one class. People vary in their skills and capabilities; they differ in the quality of work performed, and in their attention to detail. Some are able to endure longer working hours than others; some have stamina and vigilance to introduce improvements in production, and therefore can sustain a productivity level twice that of others. Some workers may be skilful in politics, and thus the welfare of the nation may hinge on their input.

Such work-related differences will produce discrepancies in value, and Marxism has admitted as much. An instance in point is the Marxist recognition that work may be classified into simple and complex types, and that an hour of the latter is worth much more than the former. When attention is directed to the issue of pay, Marxists may select one strategy form the following two:

A) Adherence to the axiom that 'each is paid according to work done'. Here different people - even within the same skill or profession - will receive varying levels of pay, resulting in class-associated discrepancies once again, and the socialist system will be coloured by a new style of class structure.

B) Borrowing the concept of 'added value' from capitalism, whereby the 'addition' embodied in more complex work goes to the State, and all workers end up having the same pay-level.

In practice, socialist societies have taken the *first* route, which leads invariably to renewed class-like variations in incomes and life-styles. Leaders in socialist countries have found it impossible to attain complete equality in earnings. For instance, income differences in the former Soviet Union were quite sharp, as it had been impractical to degrade the work done by scientists, politicians, and top military offices to that of simple menial occupations, as such a course of action would freeze ideological growth, stifle artistic and cognitive effort, and make most people go for simple and trivial pursuits, due to the sameness of pay, irrespective of the nature of work and its complexity.

This is the underlying factor which makes for discrepancies and contradictions within the socialist system. These discrepancies and contradictions were compounded through actions of the State, when repressive and intelligence agencies were set up (such the secret police), whereby distinctive privileges were handed to these organisations, in order to protect and underpin prevailing dictatorial structures. In consequence, ordinary individuals came face-to-face with the same cruel facts of their existence, as those that socialists were promising to see off for good.

As for the theoretical approach to solving the problem referred to above, this is well documented in the writings of Friedrich Engels, who states:

'How then are we to solve the whole important question of the higher wages paid for compound labour? In a society of private producers, private individuals or their families pay the costs of training the skilled worker; hence the higher price paid for trained labour power also comes first of all to private individuals; the clever slave is sold for a higher price, and the clever wage-earner is paid higher wages. In a socialistically organised society, these costs are born by society, and to it therefore belong also the fruits, the greater values produced by skilled labour. The labourer himself has no claim to extra payment. And from this, incidentally, also follows the moral that there is frequently a drawback to the popular demand of the workers for " the full product of their labour"[1]

The gist of this argument is that the higher value of complex work (as compared with simple occupations) is due to training and education, which make for a competent or professional worker. Under capitalism, the costs of such training/education is borne privately, thus enabling the individual to claim commensurate compensation. By contrast, under socialism the State has overall responsibility for education and training activities, and therefore all additional values associated with complex work must revert to the public purse. Consequently, the expert/professional worker must not earn more than what the simple worker gets.

But all this deviates completely from the real world. The extra earnings of expert people under capitalism exceed by far the costs of their training/education – as has been emphasised previously. In addition, Engels had not tackled the problem in a precise manner, as required by the alleged scientific methods of Marxist economics.

Engels had been oblivious to the fact that the costs of training/education were not included in assessing the labour effort of the skilled worker. Instead, what determined value of any good - under Marxism – was the labour expended, which was based largely – though not exclusively – on the amount of effort put in during education and/or training. In other words, the cost of education/training may be less than the value of expertise gained, i.e. the effort exerted by the trainee may exceed the visible costs of training. Such a scenario would mean that in the case of complex work, the worker would be entitled to an extra value higher than the costs of past training[2]. If in this case, the State pockets all the additional value, paying the worker what amounts to simple work-

[1] Friedrich Engels: " Herr Eugen Duhring's Revolution in Science (Anti-Duhring)" Lawrence & Wishart, London, Pg. 229 (no date given)

[2] The author does not consider here the time-value of money, which would mean that a £1 spent on training one year ago is equivalent to more than £1 in today's money. However, this does not in principle alter the logic of the argument. **(Translator's Comment)**

value only, thus a situation of 'added value' would develop similar to that under capitalism.

If we strictly apply the principles of Marxist economics, then the State ought not deduct more than the expenses it incurred in education and training[3]. If the value of the individual's effort in training/education is higher than the respective cost - as is frequently the case – then the worker should be allowed to enjoy the difference, as reflected in the value of output minus any training/education costs that had been borne by the State.

Another important point that escaped Engels concerns work complexity-cum-value resulting from *qualities* possessed by the worker, as distinct from those gained through training. A skilful and highly motivated worker may display twice the productivity of a colleague, even though both might have had the same training/education. Should we in this instance pay the more productive operative twice the going rate? If we do, variations will surface; if not then the socialist State has stolen the added value created by the efficient individual!

The upshot of all this is that the State under socialism has to make a **bitter choice** between two options, as follows:

First: applying the Marxist axiom that each receives according to contribution, in which case earning differentials will arise and may become quite sharp. This amounts to a new type of class structure under the supposedly classless umbrella of the socialist State.

Second: deviating practise from theory, whereby simple and complex work-types are equated with regard to earnings, the gifted employee with the ordinary. In this circumstance, the State would *take* 'added value' from the more efficient, in a manner similar to that practised by the capitalist, as the dictates of historical materialism would have us believe.

---

[3] Plus any relevant time-value of money. **(Translator's Comment)**

5.4 COMMUNISM

The socialist phase ends with the birth of communist society, where human beings are promised **paradise** on Earth – as spelled out by historical materialism. Two major pillars of communism may be identified here:

A) **Eradication of private property,** not merely within the context of capitalist production, but also in other areas, including non-capitalist production and ordinary consumption. This means that all means of production, as well as consumption goods, will be nationalised and become publicly-owned.

B) **Cancellation of political authority**, and final liberation of society from government.

Regarding the first point, there does ***not*** appear to be any scientific or objective basis for this. In other words, the complete eradication of private ownership does not rest on any conception of value, in a fashion similar to the rationale for establishing socialism. The Marxist laws of 'value' and 'added value' were the explanation given for dismantling capitalism and its replacement by the socialist system.

In the case of communism, the need for sweeping nationalisation is explained through the assertion that socialist society would reach a very high level of wealth, with corresponding sophistication of the forces of production. Consequently, there would be no need for owning either consumption goods or means of production, because everything is available under communism. Whatever an individual requires is there in abundance at anytime, and therefore no need arises to own anything!

This is the whole basis of distribution under communism: ***each can obtain according to need, not according to contribution***. Every person would thus take whatever he/she requires to cater for all wants, because the society's wealth is sufficient to accomplish the satisfaction of all wants.

It is hard to imagine a hypothesis that is more **indulgent** in imagination and so far-fetched in its horizons than this! How can we suppose that human beings under communism will be able to meet all their needs and wishes in a satisfactory way? How can they obtain sufficient amounts of the ever-changing multitude of goods and services, in a manner similar to their intake of air (and water), so that no scarcity of goods would arise, no competition among consumers need surface, and no one should feel the urge to appropriate anything?

It seems that communism will be an age of miracles, not least in terms of the human personality, as people will be converted into legendary or super producers. Personal and selfish motives would be extinguished within an atmosphere of omnipresent nationalisation. Parallel wonders would be created with nature itself, so much so that thriftiness and scarcity would be things of the past; instead a generous spirit would take over, providing whatever is needed for abundant output, by way of minerals, rivers and other resources.

It is indeed **unfortunate** that the leaders of the Marxist experiment have failed miserably in their attempt to create paradise on Earth. In the case of the former Soviet Union, it was declared at one juncture that socialism was accomplished, but the experiment kept oscillating between socialism and communism, until it was virtually recognised that communistic society was too ambitious and idealistic an objective, exactly as any utopian and imaginary idea, which contravenes human nature, would disintegrate so badly on the solid rock of reality.

At the beginning, the socialist revolution (in the former Soviet Union) travelled on a purely communist route, so much so that Lenin attempted to make common as many things as possible. Farmland was taken from owners, and farmers were deprived of their individual means of production. All this led to agitation and rebellion among peasants, resulting in hunger that almost destabilised the country; eventually the ruling clique had to give way by re-allowing peasants to own their means of production, in order to return the country to normal conditions.

Another attempt to outlaw private ownership in agriculture was made in the former Soviet Union in the late 1920's, producing thereby another revolt among farmers. This time round, the authorities resorted to extremely repressive measures, whereby many thousands of people were killed and jails overflowed with detainees. The hunger which ensued from the strike and turbulence in 1932 caused some six million deaths, by the admission of government sources. All this led the authorities to capitulate, so that farmers were allowed to have a piece of land, along with a cottage and some farm animals, with a proviso that the State will keep its status as the rightful owner, and that each farmer would join a State-backed co-operative, form which the individual farmer could be sacked at any time.

As for the other main cornerstone of communism (i.e. *eradication of government*), this is perhaps the most ludicrous of all communist ingredients. The whole idea relates to a view embodied in historical materialism, which claims that government is the product of class conflict, because it is an organ created by the owning class, in order to subjugate working people. On this basis, there would be no place for government within a classless setting, where all traces and vestiges of social structures have been wiped out. In consequence, government would vanish when the historical basis for its existence is present no longer.

Yet, any sane person would naturally enquire about this supposedly historical transformation from a State-linked society to one that is State-less; from socialism to the communistic phase. How can this social change come about? Does it occur through revolutionary measures or via a *coup de'etat*, so that society moves from socialism to communism at a critical point, as in the case of the transfer from capitalism to socialism? Or does this transfer materialise gradually, so that the State apparatus withers away, and shrinks slowly until it exists no more?

If transformation is supposed to take place through revolutionary and violent means, then **which** class will revolt against the government of the proletariat and put a decisive end to it? Marxism has taught us that social revolution against an existing regime must be undertaken by a social class that is not part of that regime. In this case, therefore, the revolutionary transformation to communism must be at the hands of a class/group not embodied within the socialist government. Could it be, for example, a group of capitalists?

If, on the other hand, we are to see a **gradual** transformation towards communism, then this will clash openly and directly with the laws of dialectics, on which Marxism is based. The dialectic law dealing with quantity and method stresses: qualitative changes can not be gradual, but must be abrupt, whenever change-over occurs from one situation to another. Based on this principle, Marxism believed in the inevitability of revolution at the outset of any new historical stage. How, then, could this law become null and void when we consider a society's transformation from socialism to communism?

Moreover, a peaceful change-over to communism would **contradict** the ordinary down-to-earth course of events to which we have been accustomed: how can we imagine a socialist government conceding - in a piecemeal fashion - more and more of its authority, until it repeals itself by itself ? All other governments on the face of this planet have - so far at least - attempted to hang on to power, and defend their political existence right to the last minute!

Is there anything stranger than this gradual reduction of authority, that is volunteered by the government itself, so much so that it is generous with its very existence for the sake of society's good? And, when we look at the nature of socialist systems that have existed during this (20th)century, is this not a distant cry from actual experience that we have seen and witnessed? We have learnt that a pivotal feature of the socialist stage is the setting up of a totalitarian government ... so how can such a regime be a prelude for slow death and final elimination of government?

And, finally, let us give Marxism the benefit of the doubt, by supposing that the miracle could be accomplished and that communism would be set up, whereby each person would work according to ability and receive according to need. Is there no requirement for an authority in society to determine this 'need', to accommodate conflicting wants on the same product/service, to manage work and ensure its fair and practical spread among the various sectors of the economy?

Part II

Free Market Economics

~ *Chapter Six* ~

Essential Ingredients of Capitalism

As Marxist economics is *split* into science and doctrine, free-market economics is also divided into these two parts. In the field of economic science, capitalism attempts to explain the **nature** of economic phenomena and events in an objective manner, based on analysis and logical inference. On the doctrinal front, free-marketers advocate the adoption of capitalist notions and spell out the rationale of free-market operations.

It must, however, be said that these two aspects of capitalism have been *intertwined* in much of the writings and researches produced. Yet, these two sides are different from each other, with each possessing its particular perspective, bases and measurements. If we attempted to paint any of these two aspects with the special colour of the other, a major mistake would result. Thus, scientific theories must not be covered with a doctrinal cloak; nor should doctrinal claims be coached in scientific language.

It must also be pointed out that the relationship between science and doctrine under capitalism is qualitatively different from the corresponding link under Marxism. For this important reason, the analysis of capitalism will necessarily *vary* from the parallel analysis of Marxism. A start will be made by looking at the general framework of free-market economics, so as to deal with the doctrine-science link at a later stage. Finally, capitalism will be appraised, in terms of the main doctrinal principles or ideals on which it rests.

6.1   GENERAL   FRAMEWORK   OF   THE   FREE-MARKET DOCTRINE

It is possible to summarise the chief bases of capitalism under three
main cornerstones. These clearly distinguish the capitalist doctrine,
and stamp it with its special and particular character:

First: emphasis on private ownership. While the general rule under
the Marxist doctrine is public ownership, the corresponding one for
capitalism is private ownership, in all walks of life and areas of
wealth-holding. Exceptions, however, do exist, but these must be
fully justified by their special conditions, which make public
ownership inevitable or highly desirable. Yet, as long as there is no
proven case for nationalisation, ownership must rest with the private
sector.

On this basis, capitalism adheres to the virtues of open and free
ownership, allowing owners to spread their wings to all factors of
production that can be possessed, including land, machines,
buildings, minerals and any other. Consequently, the legal system
undertakes to protect rightful owners and ensure their continued
possession and utilisation of what belongs to them.

Second: allowing each person to utilise privately-owned assets. Each
person is allowed to develop his/her wealth by various available
means and methods.   For instance, farm-land can be utilised
personally by the owner, or alternatively it can be leased to others;
terms and conditions can be imposed on other users; finally the land
can be left idle.

It is clear that the prime aim of these freedoms bestowed by the
capitalistic system on owners is to enable the individual to be the
prime mover of economic life, as no other person knows the true
interests and needs of owners better than themselves; nor are others
more capable or fitting in attaining those benefits. It is essential for
people to have sufficient manoeuvre, in order to utilise their assets
effectively and fruitfully.   People have to be free from any

intervention from the State or any other body, so as to seize opportunities in selecting avenues of investment/work, selecting the types of skills/occupations most suitable, and the methods pursued to accomplish the largest amount of gain.

Third: guaranteeing freedom of consumption and utilisation. Each person has liberty in spending their money as they please, in order to meet needs and wishes, choosing in the process the types of goods/services to consume. In certain cases, the State will intervene by prohibiting some specified goods/services, for reasons related to the public good, such as the consumption or trading of harmful drugs.

These, therefore, are the main features of the free-market doctrine, which may be summed under three essential liberties: **ownership, utilisation, and consumption**. All this brings to the surface the glaring dichotomy between the capitalist and Marxist doctrines, where the latter puts socialism as the alternative basis to replace private ownership, cancelling in its way capitalistic freedoms, which furnish the foundations of private ownership, and replacing these by State ownership and control over all fields of economic life.

A commonly-held view in this connection is that the difference between the two doctrines reflects the *different angles* from which their adherents view the individual and society at large. The capitalist doctrine focuses on the individual, valuing each person's personal motives and contribution, and regarding the single person as the catalyst, since the whole doctrine is geared towards protecting his/her interests and enhancing his/her output. In contrast, Marxism is collective in nature, rejecting selfish or personal motives, focusing instead on the need for individuals to sacrifice themselves for the society's good, regarding the latter a their focal objective. For this reason, the Marxist doctrine does not pay much regard to individual liberties, regarding them as expendable for the sake of the central theme, namely the welfare and development of the total community.

Deeper and more discerning thought, however, would reveal that both doctrines are characterised by an ***individual outlook***, because they concentrate primarily on personal and selfish considerations. On the one hand, capitalism values in lucky and successful individuals their ambitious tenacity, ensuring for them freedom of utilisation and activity in various areas, while relatively disregarding what may befall other (less fortunate) individuals by way of deprivation, backwardness and misery. The misfortune of the latter may somehow be associated with the good fortunes of the former; yet capitalists would regard that as normal, so long as both types of people are in principle enjoying the same basic liberties made available by the prevailing system.

And while capitalism provides the requisite opportunity to the lucky ones to cater for their personal needs and aspirations, cultivating in them individual ambition, drive, and instinct... Marxism directs attention the other way, i.e. towards those who have not been on the receiving end of such an opportunity, in that its doctrinal call is focused on this section of society, in order to motivate them and provoke them to take action to meet their individual needs. Marxists look upon such action as instrumental in accomplishing revolutionary change, and in advancing human history. In this process, Marxists stress to those whom they are attempting to motivate that others are depriving them of their efforts and wealth, and that they (the oppressed and deprived) cannot condone such theft and injustice, because that would be an assault on their own very existence.

It is possible, therefore, to see that the fuel utilised by Marxists is essentially the ***same*** as that adopted by capitalism, namely personal self-interest. Both doctrines adopt nurturing and satisfying self-interest as the basis of their primary appeal, while they differ in the ***type of people*** to whom their call is supposed to reach.

A doctrine that can ***truly*** be described as collective is motored by a motive of a different kind, a motive far removed from selfishness and narrow personal benefit. A collective doctrine is one that promotes in the individual a deep sense of responsibility towards society and the common good. In the process, individuals will have to concede some of the fruits of their labour and private wealth, for the sake of society, not because they have stolen from others and these others have revolted to recoup what is rightfully theirs, but because the individual has a sense of duty to make a worthwhile contribution, and this sense is an expression of the values in which the individual believes quite firmly.

The collective doctrine is one which **protects** the legitimate rights of others, as well as their welfare and happiness, not through provoking their personal aspirations and own interests, but via motivating all to care for the common good, and developing in their souls the spring of righteousness and goodness. In subsequent presentations, the nature of this doctrine will become apparent.

6.2   CAPITALISTIC DOCTRINE NOT PRODUCT OF SCIENTIFIC LAWS

At the dawn of modern economics, when the first pioneers were sowing the seeds of this social science and its fundamental structure, *two* major ideas were being mooted at the time:

The *first* asserted that economic life was moving in tune with certain **natural forces**, which dominated and determined the conditions of society in the economic sphere, exactly as other parts of the universe were dictated by various natural laws. The task of economic scientists, therefore, was to discover and identity these fundamental laws, which would explain clearly the various economic phenomena and events.

The *other* major concept, which was associated with the first, claimed that those natural laws were sufficient to secure the **welfare and happiness of humanity**, provided a free environment was made available for the working of the natural laws, and all individuals were given the liberty to practise the main capitalistic rights of ownership, utilisation and consumption.

The first idea was instrumental in establishing the initial principles of capitalistic economic science, while the second helped in evolving the associated capitalist doctrine. At the beginning, it was believed that the two notions had been inextricably linked, so much so that economic thinkers were prone to believe that limiting individual freedom, and permitting State intervention in economic affairs, were tantamount to flying in the face of nature and its prime laws, which had ensured for humanity reasonable welfare and solution of problems. Any attempt to constrain or denigrate those basic freedoms would be a crime against the fair and natural laws of this universe, thereby leading to the assertion that those fundamental laws impose the need to adhere to the capitalistic doctrine, and society would thus be required to guarantee the main capitalistic liberties[1].

To a large extent, this type of thinking now appears laughable and even childish. *No* crime would be committed if a natural law of economics is broken; in fact such an event may prove the invalidity of the respective 'law', thus depriving it of its objective or scientific connotation. Genuine natural laws would not be inoperative when the required conditions for them are present.

However, relevant conditions may alter, and therefore one cannot regard capitalistic freedoms as natural laws; nor can we view any deviations from them as a crime. The natural laws of economics will keep working unceasingly, in all types of circumstances, whatever may be the degree of liberty afforded to individuals in the areas of ownership, utilisation and consumption.

What does happen in practice is that the degree to which those laws are effectual will hinge upon the surrounding conditions and

---

[1] A case in point is the **Physiocracy** movement, which gained strong ground in France during the 18th century, and which influenced greatly the thinking of Adam Smith, the acknowledged father of classical (free-market) economics, who published his **Wealth of Nations** in 1776. **Physiocrats** believed that natural laws governed the operation of the economy, and these laws could be discovered. They asserted that free competition led to the best price, and society would benefit if individuals followed their self-interest. See:

H.Landreth & DC Colander: *'History of Economic Thought'* 3rd edition, Houghton Mifflin Company, 1994, Pp 50-56. **(Translator's Comment)**.

environment, in a similar way to how the laws of physics will differ in their effects and consequences according to the exact conditions where they are applied.

It is, therefore, necessary to study capitalistic liberties from the perspective of the opportunity they provide to individuals to realise their dignity and happiness, as well as to attain high moral values for society at large; they must not be viewed as scientific necessities ordained by natural laws – as advocates of free-market systems would have us believe. Through such a study, we can comprehend the essential difference between Marxism and capitalism, as the science-doctrine link differs noticeably between these two major systems.

As symbolised by socialism and communism, **doctrinal Marxism** is viewed as an end-product of historical materialism, which is supposed to express the natural progression of history from the Marxist standpoint. If the theory of historic materialism is correct in explaining history, then it corroborates the validity of Marxism. For this reason, a study of the scientific aspect of Marxism is an essential component of any perusal of the doctrinal side, and a necessary requirement to judge the suitability of the whole doctrine. No serious researcher can critically analyse socialism-cum-communism without looking deeply at the relevant scientific basis, as set out by the theory of historical materialism.

As for the **doctrine of capitalism**, it is definitely not a product of economic science as has been developed by early capitalist thinkers; nor does the validity of the doctrine hinge upon the correctness of the scientific side of capitalism in expounding objective facts. In essence, doctrinal capitalism depends on certain practical concepts and behavioural values, all of which should be considered when an assessment is undertaken of the doctrine.

All this helps to clarify the standpoint of the author of this book, as someone who believes in an economic doctrine, that is well differentiated from both Marxism and capitalism. However, the

Islamic assessment of Marxism is basically **different** from the angle through which capitalism is looked at.

In the case of Marxism, the whole doctrine rests on the theory of historical materialism, and hence it was necessary to critically analyse that theory. In the case of doctrinal capitalism (i.e. basic capitalistic freedoms), the doctrine does not rely on the scientific laws of economics, and hence it is not necessary to look deeply into those laws. As indicated earlier, capitalism derives its whole rationale from a group of practical concepts and behavioural values. As a result, this book need not deal with the scientific aspects of free-market economics, except in so far as that may be required to elaborate the doctrine, and to show the dividing lines between doctrine and science. This work is basically stamped with a doctrinal colour, and does not extend to the scientific aspects, except where this may be necessary to spell out the essential elements of the doctrine.

Doctrinal capitalism does not assume to itself any scientific foundation, and therefore no scientific research can be employed to critically analyse the doctrine. Nonetheless, it is possible to resort to scientific research, in order to develop a general notion of the practical and objective consequences spawned by capitalism on the social level, as well as the types of trends or developments that result from applying the economic rules (laws) of capitalism, so as to measure and assess these consequences/results **vis-à-vis** the conceptual and moral yardsticks of the researcher. The task of any scientific researcher evaluating the free-market doctrine is to give a fair profile of capitalist society, so as to appraise this profile through specific measurements. It is not the researcher's role to prove the correctness or inevitability (or otherwise) of the capitalist doctrine.

It would, for instance, be a gross mistake for the scientific researcher to regard as scientifically proven the view presented by free-market protagonists that availability of the main capitalistic liberties would furnish happiness and prosperity to all! Such a view can not be seen as scientifically correct, in the same way that an economic theorem asserting that when supply shifts upward, price will come down (if the demand schedule remains the same).

The latter theorem is bound to be correct, when price is determined in a free-market, through the forces of supply and demand. As to the former claim (i.e. provision of capitalistic freedoms leads to happiness), this is a doctrinal standpoint issued by proponents of the doctrine, and derived from their own values and moral concepts. In this case, the validity of the conclusion(s) will depend on the correctness of the premise(s), as well as the logical process of derivation.

6.3 SCIENTIFIC LAWS HAVE A DOCTRINAL FRAMEWORK

It was pointed out that doctrinal capitalism does not have a specific foundation as such, and does not derive its justification from scientific economic theories. The aim in this section is to investigate this relationship between the scientific and doctrinal parts of capitalism, in order to see how doctrinal capitalism looks upon the scientific framework within a free-market system, and influences the general trends and currents of relevant laws.

To put this issue somewhat differently, the scientific laws of free-market economics are relevant within the context of a special doctrinal setting; they are not applicable to all societies, and to every situation – as the laws of physics and chemistry are. Many of these scientific economic laws are actual truths within the social conditions where capitalism rules supreme, in all its economic, conceptual and ideological aspects, and would therefore not apply to a community where the free-market system is not adhered to.

In order to illustrate this point, let us shed some light on economic laws within the context of a capitalist economy, so as to be able to assess how – and to what degree – these can be described as objective or scientific. In this connection, scientific economic laws can be categorised within two prime groups:

First: basic laws deriving their validity from **nature** itself, as distinct from human will. A relevant example here is the **'law of overall limitation'** which stresses that total Earthly production of any item that utilises land and extracted raw materials will be limited by the total quantity available of land and relevant raw materials that can be obtained through mining.

Another example is the **'law of changing returns to scale'**. When all factors of production except one are held constant, and the quantity of this one factor is gradually increased from point zero, then at first we will experience increasing returns to scale, in the sense that for every extra unit added of this input, the extra resultant output will become higher and higher. However, a maximum level will be arrived at, after which any addition to that input will lead to lower and lower levels of extra output of the final product. In fact, if we continue to increase the quantity of the input, a point will eventually be reached where total output will start decreasing, thus indicating that over this range extra units of the input produce reductions in final production.

Such laws do not differ in their nature and objectivity from other laws of this universe, which have been discovered by the natural sciences. For this reason, natural economic laws are not associated with any doctrinal stamp; nor do they rely for their validity on any social conditions or ideological framework. The validity of these laws does not vary with time or place, so long as the natural background for production remains the same.

Second: economic laws related to **human choice**, because economic life is nothing but an expression where human will plays a pivotal role, in the full meaning of the word. If we consider here the law of 'supply and demand', where equilibrium price is determined through the dynamic impact of these two major forces, we find that this is not a totally abstract (or object-like) concept, because it does not operate separately form human consciousness – as the laws of astronomy and physics do.

For the law of supply and demand to function, market operators must respond adequately to market realities. When other things remain constant, and the demand schedule shifts upward, price will need to increase correspondingly. Yet, this result (i.e. price increase) will only come about if affected people react in a conscious and appropriate manner. This means effectively that buyers would be ready to pay the higher price, and suppliers will not sell the good/service at lower than the new equilibrium price. All this shows that such laws are *social* in nature, depending for their validity on people making rational choices.

Yet, the presence of human will in the conduct of economic transactions does not rule out the role of scientific laws in our economic life. Nor does this make scientific research impossible – as some had been quick to claim when the field of political economy was first born. This group of thinkers were of the opinion that the inevitability associated with scientific laws was diametrically opposed to liberty as embodied in human choice, so much so that when human living was subjected to stringent scientific laws, this deprived people of any freedom to act and innovate. As a result, individuals would become similar to materialistic objects, influenced and adapted mechanically in accord with scientific laws, which dominate the conduct of their economic lives.

Such a standpoint hinges on an erroneous view of human liberty, as well as embodying a perverted sense of the link between liberty and choice – on the one hand – and those laws, on the other. The existence of scientific laws in people's life does not entail the loss of individual liberty and power of choice. In effect, these laws explain how human beings utilise their liberties in the economic sphere, without any loss of human will or freedom of choice.

However, scientific laws in the field of economics need to be differentiated from scientific laws in other spheres of this universe, in that the former are related to human choice, and impacted on by influences which leave their mark on people's consciousness, thus permeating all factors that play a part in a person's choice and inclinations.

And, it is only natural that human will – which is tackled by those laws – will be determined according to the individual's thoughts and the type of doctrine prevalent in society, as well as the nature of current legislation which limit people's conduct and thinking process. All these factors tend to shape the individual's decisions and mould his/her practical standpoint; a change in these factors will produce corresponding alterations in the person's opinions and choices.

The upshot of all this is that the general scientific laws which explain the economic aspect of life will differ among cultures, communities, and even between various epochs for a given society. In many cases, it is not possible to elaborate a general law for all humanity, to encompass economic life irrespective of the pertinent doctrinal, ideological and spiritual framework. It would, therefore, be scientifically incorrect to expect that the exercise of human choice will result in undertaking activities and producing goods/services in all societies, exactly as happens in the case of a capitalist economy, where relevant laws of political economy have been well established. As long as societies continue to vary in their ideological, doctrinal and spiritual frameworks, it is necessary for these frameworks to be taken as given parameters when conducting scientific research; here it becomes possible to arrive at research fruits which duly mirror the prevalent laws within those varying frameworks.

As a relevant example here, we can look at the concept of self-interest, being the solid basis on which much of classical economic thinking was built. In essence, Adam Smith and his fellow classical economists regarded the pursuit of self-interest as the driving force that propelled individuals and provided economic activity with the requisite momentum, and that such a pursuit by individuals would serve the public good, since the latter was the sum total of all individual benefits in any given community. Consequently, classical thinkers set about unveiling the scientific laws governing such a society; indeed their fundamental supposition was valid within the context of a capitalist European setting, along with concomitant ideological and spiritual conditions, that produced certain behavioural and practical criteria.

It must, nonetheless, be recognised that any society may witness major changes in life-style and economic circumstances, if this fundamental supposition (i.e. prime pursuit of self-interest) was altered. In this case, a new type of society will come about, which is different from a capitalist system. Here, the general demeanour of individuals will be different, with new concepts and values emerging. All this is not a mere hypothesis, but very much a realistic fact, as we do notice that societies vary, in terms of the factors which determine individual behaviour and practical values.

A comparison between the capitalistic system and the society that Islam called for, and had brought it to existence, would illustrate the point here. Under the Islamic umbrella, ordinary mortals lived, but they differed substantially and noticeably from those living under capitalism, in terms of their general demeanour and practical outlook to life, as well as in terms of their spiritual and ideological make-up.

As both a religion and a special doctrine for living, Islam had its profound impact on economic events and social setting, despite the fact that the religion *per se* did not contain any scientific analysis of economics. However, Islam dealt with the main planks of the economic and social make-up, as it related to human beings themselves, along with their cognitive notions about life, their motives and aims, so much so as to mould the individual in a special ideological and spiritual setting.

Although the Islamic experiment in this regard can be viewed as relatively short, it did result in the most wonderful consequences ever witnessed by men and women. That experiment proved that it was possible to raise human standards to levels, and broaden thinking horizons to extents, that could not be imagined by individuals living in a capitalist framework, who had always been fully covered up to their necks with materialistic concepts and requirements.

With the little information that history provides us by way of the results of that Islamic experiment, and the allied wonders it spawned, we can visualise the potentialities for goodness treasured deep down within the human soul, along with the missionary zeal released by Islam, which harnessed those potential energies in the service of major human issues. A case in point is the reported story of a group of poor people who raised with Prophet Mohammad the matter of rewards (from Almighty Allah) earned by rich individuals for their 'donations to charitable causes'. The Prophet's response was that even relatively poor people could 'give alms, recite (or whisper) praises and glories of Allah, as well as persuade (or direct) others to do good and refrain from evil ...' All these things would invite generous compensation from Allah, in a fashion similar to that gained by the wealthy for their charitable donations.

It is noteworthy that these Muslims who mooted the point with the Prophet did not want wealth for its own sake, or as a conduit for power or prestige; nor did they seek it in order to cater for their personal desires. In essence, they required it because it was hard for them to see the wealthy surpassing them on the road of righteousness and moral values, through sheer good work and social philanthropy. All this reflects the place of wealth in Islam, and the nature of the Muslim individual, within the context of a total and integrated Islamic approach to life.

In a piece where Al-Shatibi[2] describes leases and commercial transactions prevalent within early Islamic society, the writer says:

'You would find them taking very little by way of profit or rent, in the context of commercial transactions or leases, so that the other party would get out of the deal as much as possible. They therefore went a long way in providing advice, over and above what was essential, as if they were agents for the other party, rather than

---

[2] A recognised authority on Islamic history. (**Translator's Comment**)

serving their own interest. In fact, they viewed a concentrated push for their own benefit as verging on the deceit of others'.

Another relevant piece is from the writings of Mohammad ibn Ziyad when spelling out co-operation and mutual assistance within an Islamic society. He writes: ' a guest would sometimes arrive, where the host is unprepared. The latter would take the initiative and appropriate a prepared meal in a neighbour's vessel, which was slowly being readied on fire. When the (neighbouring)owner of the vessel enquires about its whereabouts, the host confirms that he had taken it in order to serve the guest, whereby the vessel-owner retorts by saying "May Allah bless you with it"'.

Thus, it is possible to realise the positive and effective role of Islam, in impacting on the general economic current of life, in that individuals themselves are remoulded, and new spiritual and ideological conditions are created. Simultaneously, we can understand the gravity of the error of allowing a society enjoying such characteristics and ingredients to be subjected to the laws which govern a capitalistic community, which is overwhelmed by selfishness and materialistic notions.

In this regard, let us look at a certain law pertaining to income distribution and price determination. A classical law on income distribution is the so-called **'iron laws of wages'** which stressed that labour wages should merely cover the bare essentials of life, while the other elements of gross revenue should be devoted to other factors of production, including land rent, business profits etc. If payments to labour exceeded this bare subsistence level, then wage-earners' standard of living should improve, and they would produce more children. As the higher birth rate would feed into the labour supply, the result would be a noticeable fall in wages to bring them to the 'natural' level. On the other hand, if wages were below the subsistence level, then poverty and disease would become rife among labourers; many will perish; labour supply will decrease. The eventual outcome of this scenario is that wage levels would go up to the 'natural' level[3].

Such thinking was presented by classical (free-market) economists to explain actual facts in a scientific fashion, and as a ***natural law*** of economics[4]. In fact, this law is only applicable within definite limits, and in the context of capitalist systems where no social security system exists, while wage levels are left totally to the whims of supply and demand.

The iron law of wages would ***not*** rule in a society where a reasonable social-security set-up exists, to guarantee a minimum living standard for working people and their families, as would be the case in an Islamic society, or where the market system is suspended - as would be the case under socialism. In these cases, a concept such as the iron law of wages would not be operational, as it would in a classical-like capitalist system. It is clear from all this that the general framework of capitalist economics has a definitive doctrinal colour, and does not enjoy the sacred nature of absolute scientific laws.

---

[3] The **'wages fund doctrine'** along with the associated **'iron law of wages'** were evolved by classical economists, mainly David Ricardo, Adam Smith and Thomas Malthus. The 'wage fund doctrine' asserted that in any enterprise only a specific sum of gross income must be devoted to the payment of labour wages. It must however be said that those ideas attracted much criticism from reformist and humanist thinkers, such as John Stuart Mill, not to mention socialist writers such as Karl Marx. See:
H.Landreth & DCColander: **'History of Economic Thought'** 3rd edition, Houghton Mifflin Co., 1994, Pp. 91-105. **(Translator's Comment).**
[4] It has to be said that supporters of this line of thinking still exist in the industrialised countries of the West, and perhaps in other regions as well, although it is rather difficult to gauge precisely the extent and depth of this support. **(Translator's Comment).**

~ *Chapter Seven* ~

Main Values of Free-Market Economics

As has been noted in the previous chapter, the cornerstone of doctrinal capitalism is **individual liberty** in the economic field, in all relevant manifestations of ownership, utilisation and consumption. Personal freedom is the springboard, from which all relevant rights and doctrinal values, advocated by proponents of the free-market system, emanate. In fact, all scientific laws of the capitalist system are nothing but a reflection of the objective details which develop within the context of this freedom.

Consequently, it is necessary to critically analyse the **essence** of individual liberty, and look at its ideological seeds, along with the main values and ideas on which it is based. The question that presents itself at the outset concerns the ***need*** for a society to be built on the foundation of economic liberty. In this regard, how did the right of human beings to be free evolve?

In order to answer this question, we need to understand that individual liberty - according to capitalist thinking - is ***linked*** to other ideas and values, from which the concept of individual liberty derives its very existence within the whole doctrine, along with its central characteristic as a social and humanistic imperative for human race as a whole.

In one respect, the notion of individual liberty relates to the alleged close relationship between personal interest and the good of society in general. Classical economists believed in the **invisible hand** which prompted each person to further their innate interest, while the 'general good' is served through such endeavour. As the latter was thought to be merely the sum total of the interests of all individuals within a given society, the capitalist doctrine insists on securing the freedom to every individual, so that the personal motive will lead to the attainment of private interests, and this will necessarily and by implication serve the collective cause. Therefore, personal liberty is simply a means to accomplish the common good, and ensure that society will acquire what it aspires to, by way of welfare and progress.

In another vein, personal liberty is intertwined with **economic development**, because economic freedom is thought to be the best motive to drive the productive forces. In other words, personal liberty is seen as the most effective channel to harness people's energies and potentialities in the service of overall production, so as to augment the social wealth of any nation. This can in fact be related to the previous point, because we are dealing here with one major aspect of common good, namely developing social production and furthering general welfare .

In yet a third context, personal liberty links with the alleged **sanctity of freedom** as expounded by adherents of capitalist philosophy. Here, the idea assumes an essentially moral connotation, whereby advocates of capitalism utter rather murky notions, which are not totally clear. They tend to repeat that 'freedom' is generally a human prerogative, expressing in a practical fashion the dignity of mankind. 'Freedom' in this context is not a mere conduit for social welfare or increasing output, but a necessary condition to ensure adequate value for all human beings, and to emphasise their proper and natural existence.

If we take the first two concepts mentioned above, then economic liberty has a clear **objective**, owing to the results and impacts which flow from it in real life. If, however, we consider the third concept, then economic liberty is merely one aspect of freedom in the general sense, whereby the latter possesses an intrinsic value dictated by people's consciousness of their dignity and human essence.

Each of the above three notions requires deep analysis and ample study. The remainder of this chapter will undertake this task.

7.1   FREEDOM AND THE COMMON GOOD

The idea of unleashing personal freedom rests on the belief that individual motives will serve common interests, and that general social welfare will be attained through the pursuit of private gain. When economic liberty is provided to all individuals, then people will endeavour to further their own interests, and this will lead to the accomplishment of public interest and welfare.

Initially, classical (free-market) economists imagined that the welfare of society did not require the safeguarding or preservation of any moral or spiritual values, and people did not need to be instilled with any such concepts. Each individual - even those who know nothing about these philosophical ideas - would strive to maximise their own private advantage, if sufficient liberty was guaranteed for them to work as they pleased. This will advance the interests of society as a whole, and hence it is possible to *dispense* with any function presented by moral/spiritual values.

However, it would be wrong to infer from this that a capitalist society would be completely *devoid* of moral or spiritual notions. Yet, the capitalist doctrine *per se* does not recognise the necessity for such values, in order to protect the community's interests. People need not adhere to moral values, but as individual liberty is guaranteed, every person has a choice to stick to them or reject them, as they wish.

A further point put forward by advocates of capitalism is that economic freedom will create the scope for **competition** among businesses, thus ensuring that business-people will always stay vigilant to developments in the market-place, so as to secure the survival of the business, as well as to improve and expand it as far as possible. Competition is the best means to guarantee that businesses will stay efficient, and advances in productivity will be forthcoming, so as to withstand the rigours of the market and the onslaught of rivals.

This type of business environment will be conducive to continual technical up-grading and innovation, as well as searching for all possible means to reduce costs, improve product quality and lowering selling prices. Such events will not have the characteristic of one-off phenomena, but will keep recurring, so much so that only the fittest of businesses will survive, while less efficient ones will wither away and disappear. In the context of the capitalist system, therefore, competition will be a scourge over business, weeding out the lazy-cum-inefficient and securing longevity to those firms owned/managed by the competent and astute.

The argument runs that such a business culture will *serve* the socio-economic aims of society, because scientific, technological and managerial brains will be exercised to the full, while human needs will be catered for at the lowest costs possible. Whey, therefore, do we need to burden entrepreneurs or managers with a special behavioural setting or a given spiritual orientation? While the deep-seated interest of this class of people guarantees their motivation to serve themselves, and in turn attain public good, there no need to fill their ears with moral advice and lectures on the public good, as long as the bottom line is secured through a free and open society, where competition is a pivotal feature. Also, it is not necessary to ask business-people and other wealthy individuals to contribute to philanthropy, and to be concerned for public welfare, because they will do this in any case, due to their vested private interest as members of the whole society, in which they live and function.

It would be difficult - indeed ludicrous - to accept all this narrative about intertwining between general interest and personal motives, within the context of a capitalist system. The history of capitalism is overflowing with miseries and catastrophes that may be viewed as unprecedented, in addition to sharp contradictions between private and public interests. The shelving of spiritual-cum-moral values has caused a huge vacuum, so much so that capitalist society has become rampant with a variety of injustices, excesses and greed.

Through tracing the empirical history of capitalism, it is possible to identify many outrages consequent upon this alleged freedom. The concept of *capitalistic freedom* has been employed to refute all moral and spiritual requirements, and this has had grave repercussions on economic life, as well as on the spiritual well-being of society. Moreover, relationships between capitalist societies and other nations have been strongly and negatively impacted. All this had convinced many capitalist enthusiasts that their system needed adjustment and renovation, so as to scrap much of the original features and hide the scars from the surface. The result is that capitalism in its true and pure colours has become more a doctrine of the past than a living system that is actually experienced in practice.

With regards to the normal current of economic life under capitalism, absolute liberty is often viewed as a highly effective weapon in the hands of the powerful, in order to ready the path and pave the way to gain wealth and prestige, irrespective of any harm or detriment befalling others. Because people vary in terms of mental and physical endowments, as well as in the types of opportunities available to them, it is only to be expected that they will differ in the extent and avenues of economic freedom that will actually be utilised. Inevitably, these differences will mean that the rich and powerful will apply the whole legal and administrative framework to their full advantage, as this framework will be regarded by them as the solid manifestation of liberty in society. Others, meanwhile, will not see much for them in this system.

In its purest and barest form, capitalistic freedom does not recognise the need for any type of control or monitoring by an external (e.g. religious or State) agency/body.   Consequently, those who are relegated to secondary positions in the battle of life will lose all pretences to security or dignity, remaining at the mercy of the strong and influential, who know no moral or spiritual limits to their 'freedom', and whose calculations are dictated by the requirements of their own private interests.   In fact, there is ample evidence to corroborate the contention that people have been subjected to much encroachment and humiliation, as a result of this capitalistic freedom.

Human beings have become just like any article in the marketplace, with their value determined by supply and demand.   Human life itself has often become a hostage to the laws of the market, dictated effectively by the operation of the 'iron law of wages'.   According to this 'law' of classical economics, when the supply of manpower increases, wage levels would fall, thereby mortality rates go up. Capitalists would take advantage of such a situation, in order to lower costs and raise profits, remaining oblivious of any miseries brought to the masses of working people.

Under these circumstances, poverty and starvation would be acceptable, so long as liberty is guaranteed to the strong and influential, with a dim light at the end of the tunnel for the weak and dispossessed.   This faint hope – according to the 'iron law of wages' – is the anticipated reduction in the size of the workforce, who are likely to gain back their employment, along with a rise in their pay to a mere subsistence level!

This, therefore, is the supposed harmony of interest between private pursuits and the common good, within the context of capitalist freedom.   However, capitalists themselves have had their belief shaken in this alleged harmony, preferring instead to place limits on liberty through certain checks and guarantees.   And, if this is the nature of economic life under a purely capitalist regime, then the damage afflicting the spiritual core of the whole society is quite serious and ever-lasting.   Charitable tendencies and philanthropy will become constrained, while notions of selfishness and greed will be widespread, with the struggle for survival much in evidence, instead of a willingness to co-operate and assist.

Even if we suppose that personal motives will secure the interest of the society at large, there remains the issue of relations with other nations/communities. Will the legendary harmony between private and public interest within the capitalist system be replicated in the context of the relationship with other human groupings? Granted that the belief in unfettered freedom is entrenched within a free-market system, what restraints are there to prevent the leaders of such a society from recruiting various other human groupings to serve their narrow interests and to enslave them for the sake of these objectives?

The historical facts of capitalism provide a sufficient answer to this question. Humanity had endured cruelly and enormously at the hands of capitalist societies, due to the virtual absence of any moral/spiritual content within the latter, and their special approach to life. Many shameful testimonies will stay as negative hallmarks on the face of modern materialistic civilisation, and as proof that economic freedom by itself - without any concomitant moral guidelines - will represent the most detrimental kind of weaponry used by humans against their brethren, causing untold miseries and destruction.

A consequence of this freedom has been the frenetic race among European nations to colonise and subjugate weak and tranquil nations, exploiting them in the service of capitalist production. The history of Africa by itself presents a chapter in that feverish rush, resulting in an avalanche of misery to the inhabitants of the black continent. Several European countries (e.g. Britain, France, Holland) imported huge numbers of indigenous African people, and sold them in the slave markets, thus enabling fat capitalists to become even fatter.

It is well documented that slave merchants had resorted to setting African villages on fire, to force their peaceable folks to flee in fear for their lives, so that traders would hunt them down and herd them as chattel into ships for market destinations. These campaigns and atrocities continued unabated till the 19th century, when Britain took the initiative to terminate this activity through promulgating international treaties banning the slave trade. However, this endeavour itself had a capitalist aura, as it was not related to any realistic moral or spiritual values, because available evidence indicates that the action was not taken for a noble cause.

The evidence is clear. Britain made great fuss about piracy, sending her enormous navy to monitor African coasts, so as to put a final stop to the slave trade. However, the British fleet soon found its way to the western part of Africa, conquering substantial swathes of territory. In effect, therefore, this merely replaced one type of subjugation by another; slavery destined for the markets of Europe were superseded by direct and glaring colonial rule. Is it possible to say, then, that capitalistic freedom represents a magical solution or a panacea, which performs its momentous role, irrespective of any moral or spiritual considerations, in transforming people's pursuits of their own private interests into a mechanism that secures the attainment of general good and social welfare?

7.2   FREEDOM AND ECONOMIC DEVELOPMENT

This is the second major notion on which capitalist freedom is based. It involves an error in understanding the results of capitalist freedom, while another mishap relates to estimating the social value of output in society and general welfare.

Firms operating within a capitalist system cannot be viewed as atomistic units which are able to compete with one another on equal footing, so as to preserve a truly (or perfectly) competitive marketplace and ensure that production of various products/services is constantly being upgraded, both quantitatively and qualitatively. As well known, businesses vary widely in terms of size, quality of management, technology, market presence, economic sector and so on. Fierce competition often leads to the demise of weak businesses, while mergers or acquisitions occur in other instances, thereby resulting in the rise and dominance of absolute or relative monopolies.

Such processes will have the inevitable consequence of *killing off competition*, and its potential benefits in the area of economic development. Therefore, it is only for a limited period that perfect or near-perfect competition will go hand in hand with capitalist freedom. Once that epoch is past, relative or absolute monopolistic power will take over, as long as a free reign is allowed to total capitalistic freedom.

The other fundamental error relates to how output is *assessed and valued* in general, and the consequent welfare to the community. Let us suppose that a free competitive environment will continue under capitalism, and this will lead to economic development, thereby resulting in least-cost production. All this does not secure the happiness of the community, but shows simply that society is able to improve and expand output of all goods and services − if the relevant assumptions are correct. In terms of social welfare, this is not everything!

As the doctrine is required to ensure maximum (or at least reasonable) welfare for the general community, this result is a serious drawback of capitalism. Social welfare hinges to a large degree on the distribution of wealth and income in society, as well on the amount output (income) generated and wealth accumulated[1]. A major problem of (pure) capitalism is that it is incapable in securing efficient distribution of wealth and income, in order to secure an appropriate level of social welfare and happiness to all, due to the

---

[1] Another possibly serious criticism of capitalism is that certain activities may be allowed (whether implicitly or explicitly) that are wasteful or detrimental to the general good. **(Translator's comment).**

vital dependence on the price mechanism as the linchpin of the whole system.

Those who for any reason are unable to put down the price of goods required will simply have to stay without, and may thus degenerate or perish. People who face this kind of fate are those who are unable to participate fully in the process of production, or who do not get the relevant opportunity, or where others (e.g. competitors) have slammed all openings in their way. For this reason, unemployment is a major human catastrophe associated with the capitalist system, because when a working person is made redundant – for whatever reason – then he/she may not be able even to procure the bare essentials of life, leading inexorably to a catalogue of hunger, disease and misery. These individuals will not have their proper share of the output produced or wealth available, no matter how abundant either of these may be in absolute terms.

It is therefore possible to argue that any excessive praise or commendation of capitalist efficiency, and the system's resilience in attaining productivity growth, is essentially a smoke screen and a barrier to cloak the dark side of the system. Capitalism – especially in its bare doctrinal theme – delivers a cruel judgement on those who remain deprived and dispossessed, through the sheer operation of the distribution system. This system is hard and merciless on those who do not know the password, and who do not manage to acquire the magic pieces of paper/metal – money!

The conclusion must, therefore, be that the ***mere maximisation*** of output/wealth can not be a moral or practical justification for allowing virtually all means and avenues which provide momentum to the forces of production to operate in a dynamic and unconstrained fashion. This may guarantee plentiful production, but as has been noted, this stops far short from catering fully or adequately for general social welfare.

7.3 FREEDOM AND HUMAN DIGNITY

This is the *third* factor underpinning personal freedom. Here, liberty is assessed from an individual's angle, and given a purely moral value, because it is regarded as both the essential and outward expression of **dignity**. In addition, freedom makes possible self-fulfilment, which gives worth and content to life itself.

It must be pointed out that there are two types of freedom, viz. natural and social. *Natural freedom* is endowed by nature itself, while 'social liberty' is provided by the social system, which guarantees it to all members. Each of these two types has its own special features, which need to be spelled out and separated from those of the other type.

'Natural freedom' is a quintessential ingredient of any human being's whole existence. Indeed, it is a basic phenomenon that is common to all living entities, though varying in extent according to the vitality, development and resilience of each species. For this reason, human beings have a much larger claim to freedom than any other category of living entities. The stronger the claim of any living entity to life, the larger is the measure of freedom enjoyed by that category.

In order to assess the true nature of natural freedom, we need to notice the conduct of lifeless objects. **Nature** delineates a rigid framework for these objects, and it is impossible for them to deviate from that given pattern. As an example, stones have a certain nature and a set pattern of conduct, in accord with general global laws. We do not expect a stone to move in any direction, unless power is exerted to make it move; it definitely will not move or travel, except in the direction dictated by the pressure/power in question. Nor can we imagine that a stone would retract to avoid collision with another object. The stone is, therefore, devoid of any type of positive power or the ability to make adaptations, and hence it has no chance of enjoying natural liberty.

Living creatures, on the other hand, do not assume a negative posture vis-à-vis outside conditions or the surrounding environment. Nor is their stand limited in one definitive direction, where any deviation is unthinkable. Organisms that are alive possess the ability to adjust, and can innovate new ways to deal with given situations if the normal method was unsuitable. Such positive energy is the indicator of natural freedom, because nature has placed various alternatives at the disposal of the living entity, so that the latter could select – in each given case – the most appropriate option.

If we consider botanic organisms, which may be viewed as being at the lower end of the ladder of living entities, we find that they do have some energy or freedom at a primary or basic level. Many plants do change direction when encountering a barrier that prevents them from extending on a particular path, so much so that we can speak of a limited process of 'self-adjustment' and 're-orientation'.

Animal creatures come one stage higher up, on the ladder of life, as they are endowed with a wider span of liberty and energy. An animal usually has a fairly broad set of options, from which choice may be made on the basis of appropriateness with inclinations and desires. While a stone does not deviate from a given direction when thrown away, and plants can change course within rigid limits, animals can go in various directions under each given circumstance, as needs and inclinations require. The field allowed by nature for the exercise of animal activity is greatly more diverse and richer than any degree of choice afforded to plant entities.

The highest level of freedom is attained by humans, owing to the enormously large field of practical choice provided to them by nature. Instinctive propensities and desires place ultimate constrains on the field in which animals operate, so that animal liberty is used merely within those limits. Those instinctive inclinations and desires do not have the same status or crucial effect in the case of humans, because of the latter's complex make-up. Human beings have a special physiological and psychological composition, whereby they can control or conquer their desires, or at least lessen their impact.

Humans are free agents, in allowing themselves to follow their desires and obeying them, or alternatively opposing them.

This natural freedom that members of the human race enjoy is well and truly an *essential* ingredient of humanity itself, as it expresses the vital energy embodied in it. Humanity detached from this freedom is a meaningless concept. It is clear that this notion of freedom falls outside the realm of doctrinal research, as it has no doctrinal colour. Natural freedom is a gift from God (Allah), as distinct from being an endowment by, or a characteristic of, any given doctrine, and hence it should not be studied in a doctrinal context.

Freedom that has a doctrinal dimension *characterises* capitalism, and occupies the fundamental basis in its overall structure; it is **'social freedom'**. This is the freedom that the individual gains from society – not from nature. It is linked to the whole social existence of humans, and permeates all doctrinal and social studies.

A clear dichotomy between *natural* and *social* freedom will enable us to understand the error in giving 'social' freedom the same characteristics as 'natural' liberty, and in saying that the freedom made possible through the capitalist doctrine is an essential part of humanity and a vital element in its whole structure. This view reflects a lack of differentiation between 'natural freedom', as a prime element of human existence, and 'social freedom' as a major issue requiring in-depth study. It is important to determine the role and contribution of the latter concept, in building a coherent community that is at ease with itself and well contented.

Let us now look at 'social freedom' as described above, so as to assess how capitalism would look at it. An in-depth perusal of 'social freedom' reveals that it possesses a significant *core*, as well as an *outward appearance*. These two aspects may respectively be termed as 'realistic essence' and 'outward cloak' of freedom. Alternatively, they may be referred to as *real* and *nominal* freedom.

Taking first the 'realistic essence' of social freedom, this can be described as the ability acquired by individuals from society, so as to accomplish certain actions. The clear implication here is that the community at large provides each member with requisite means and conditions for those actions/accomplishments. When the social set-up is such that a person is enabled to possess the market value of a certain type of goods (e.g. own a home), while that good is made available in the market where no dominant supplier/buyer is permitted to operate, individuals become truly free to purchase that good. It is clear that under these circumstances, every person enjoys the social conditions upon which hinges the proper acquisition of that article. In contrast, when the socio-economic fabric is such that most people can not acquire the ability to buy the article and/or the article is not made available in a genuinely free market, then *real* liberty does not exist.

On the other hand, 'outward' or 'nominal' freedom does not embody all the above conditions or surrounding environment. In theory, individuals may be able to buy a good or an article, but when they are deprived of the practical capability of obtaining the necessary price, then this is a freedom *in name* only. 'Nominal freedom' means that there is no formal bar on an individual taking a relevant course of action, yet practicalities entail the effective outcome of making that alternative a virtual on-option for most or all members of society.

People are outwardly free to purchase ordinary pens, as they are to acquire a 100-million dollar enterprise, so long as the social system allows both courses of action. However, when we look at the latter (i.e. acquisition of a 100-million dollar business), then the vast majority of people are free to do this in name only. Most people are incapable of such a purchase, due to the limited opportunity open to them and lack of conducive requirements. Yet, society has in principle rendered this liberty, which may be termed as an 'outward freedom'.

All that said, 'outward freedom' may not be as hollow as this may sounds, as it can have a positive meaning under certain circumstances. A business person (or a small firm) who is showing success, and attaining gradual progress, can indeed bid for a larger business/company, thus indicating in reality the existence of respective liberty. For it is possible for the business-person/small firm to succeed in this bid and acquire a much a large corporate entity, if an effective strategy, along with a well-rounded plan, is put in motion.

In this instance, the nominal freedom to acquire a much larger corporation has a positive connotation, because while the target firm would probably not submit outright to any type of take-over proposal, the would-be acquirers possess the chance to put their skills to the test and undertake various activities/steps to reach their objective. The ingredient that is absent in this 'nominal' freedom is any guarantee from society of the requisite means to procure the resources needed. Such a guarantee is the very essence of realistic or meaningful freedom, which is denied by 'outwardly' or 'nominal' freedom.

In consequence, it can be argued that nominal social freedom is not always devoid of real content: it is a tool or a conduit to provoke latent individual energies and capabilities, so as to harness and direct them on the path of attaining ambitious targets, despite the absence of any assurance of success to punters/entrepreneurs, who dare for the fruits of higher things. It is important to recognise that 'nominal freedom' is a necessary pre-requisite for the ability to succeed. In our example, the mediocre business-person/firm would not reach the stage of realistic ability to purchase a large corporation, had there not been an initial opening in the form of nominal freedom, which makes it possible for 'minnows' or small players to try their luck and exercise their intelligence to attain the status of 'big fish'. At the same time, for the many who fail in their endeavours, or who feel unable even to contemplate higher things, freedom remains purely 'nominal' or 'outwardly' in nature.

It must be said here that the capitalist doctrine adopts the concept of 'nominal social freedom', believing that this is the embodiment of a sound notion of liberty. As to the parallel concept of 'genuine liberty', capitalists would argue that it corresponds to the degree to which people are able and willing to make use of available freedom, rather than being the 'real freedom' itself. As a result, those who adhere to pure capitalist doctrine are not truly concerned with providing individuals with the ability to enjoy realistic freedom, and less so with granting them genuine freedom.

Instead, each person would seize opportunities as they arise, and to the extent that their drive and capabilities urge them. The system itself merely furnishes nominal freedom, permitting members to practise all types of economic activities, in their strife to accomplish personal and corporate goals, while simultaneously rejecting any social authority which attempts coercion or applies pressure in any field of life.

It is therefore clear that capitalism assumes a rather negative stance towards the notion of 'realistic freedom' and a positive one vis-à-vis 'nominal freedom'. In other words, the capitalist system is not committed to providing the first, but it guarantees the second to each and every member of society. Two factors may be put forward by proponents of capitalism, to justify this cardinal orientation regarding the fundamental concept of liberty.

Firstly: any social doctrine can not fully guarantee the true and full meaning of liberty to every individual member of society, through granting them all necessary means to attain their targets. Many individuals lack any special skills or capabilities necessary to reach their objectives; it is impossible for the doctrine to make a genius out of a straw person, or to push an unbalanced individual to be 'a high-flier'.

By the nature of things, certain objectives cannot be accomplished by everybody. It is unreasonable, for example, for each and every individual to become head of State; nor can the system secure for every person the ability to actually assume the presidency/monarchy/premiership of State/government. What is reasonable is that opportunity is available to all to compete and exercise their energies/intelligence within the field of politics and economics. A few will achieve spectacular success and grab the summit; some will only reach half-way; others will be utter losers. What is important is that each individual is responsible for his/her own outcome in this battle of life, and must bear the full responsibility for any success or failure.

Secondly: capitalists would argue that the adoption of the concept of realistic freedom would have the effect of seriously weakening the feeling of responsibility by each individual, dampening in the process his/her drive and resolve, as these qualities are essential for energy and vigilance. When the system guarantees success to the individual, self-reliance will be fatally diminished, and no genuine attempt will be made to harness and utilise potential skills and latent capabilities.

Both of the above reasons are correct to some extent, but not quite in the manner set out by supporters of capitalism, whereby the concept of genuine liberty is refuted outright. The guarantee of a certain *minimum* of realistic freedom within the economic sphere is neither idealistic nor impractical. Such a limited amount of security should not stifle abilities and kill off any potential for growth and increased sophistication among men and women, so long as the upper echelons of society can only be reached through open competition. A social 'safety net' would thus leave the road wide open for individuals to exert their efforts and develop their sense of achievement.

It can therefore be asserted that capitalism can not claim that it is impossible to provide any guarantee of real liberty, however limited this may be. Nor can its proponents allege that such provision will paralyse energy or human drive, as long as avenues above this minimum stay wide open for rivalry, in order to nurture capabilities and develop pertinent skills.

The rather negative capitalistic orientation towards genuine freedom and associated concept of 'social security' are a necessary product of the doctrine's positive view towards nominal freedom. When the early advocates of capitalism took up the latter and built the whole system on this basis, it became necessary to refute the idea of social security and assume a negative view of genuine liberty, as the two concepts of liberty are rather inconsistent.

Genuine liberty would ***not*** be available in a society adhering passionately to the principle of nominal freedom, where people would enjoy this in all spheres, including the right of business-people to employ others and lay them off, as well as the ability of rich individuals to make use of their wealth in accord with own interests.

This scenario has no room for job security, or reasonable living conditions for the sick, deprived and infirm, as such guarantees clash openly with the freedom granted to business-owners and wealthy individuals.   The **choice**, therefore, is between ***two*** primary alternatives, thus:

A) granting the business-class and financiers the prerogative to conduct their affairs as they see fit, with the consequence that only nominal liberty would be provided, while any effective security relating to work or living conditions would be non-existent.

B) Provision of genuine work/life-style guarantees, resulting in significant limitations on the powers of business firms and people with money.

In practice, supporters of pure or classical capitalism have adhered to the first model of liberty, leaving to one side the notion of genuine or realistic freedom. In contrast, socialists have claimed to subscribe to the opposite view, in the sense that Marxist socialism discarded nominal freedom through instituting a dictatorial regime with absolute authority, alleging thereby that realistic or genuine freedom would be secured via this route, by assuring citizens of work opportunities and a minimum standard of decent living.

It can thus be argued - rather crudely - that each of these two rival theories (i.e. Marxism and capitalism) took one aspect of freedom and abandoned the other. No real accommodation between these polarised viewpoints has been possible, except within the context of Islam, whereby a framework is provided to cater for both types/aspects of liberty, because any society would require both. The essence of freedom is provided via securing a decent standard of living to all members of society, without allowing any person to practise their personal liberty in contravention of this secured 'safety net'. At the same time, nominal freedom is preserved as well. It is only during the 20th century that relevant experiments in non-Muslim countries have been undertaken, in the course of accommodating and blending the two types of freedom, due to the miserable failure of the (classic) capitalist model.

All the above leads to the surfacing of a major issue concerning *the values on which nominal liberty is based* within the capitalist framework. It can be said that advocates of capitalism have sacrificed the essence of freedom and the security it brings, for the sake of those values. It is important to exclude here any attempts to justify nominal freedom by involving certain objective-sounding social criteria, such as the need to maximise total production or general welfare. Such justifications/criteria have been looked at over previous pages of this book and have been found wanting and deficient.

Moreover, it may be argued that liberty is part of the total being of human existence; any deprivation of this freedom would be degrading, whereby men and women would suffer a loss of dignity, which is their differentiating characteristic from other creatures. Expressions such as these are thin on the ground, and lack the rigour of scientific analysis needed in looking at the intrinsic value of freedom.

Humans are distinguished clearly from other living entities by their possession of 'natural' liberty, *not* 'social' freedom. The former is an *inherent* ingredient of human existence; the latter is a *social* phenomenon that may be granted or denied - according to the type of prevailing doctrine-cum-system.

It may also be claimed that liberty in its social connotation is a normal or innate tendency within people, reflecting one of their essential requirements. As an extension of their natural liberty, people are prone to be as socially free as possible within the community where they exist. In consequence, it is a function of any socio-economic doctrine to recognise the variety of ideas and tendencies among people, and attempt to satisfy them to the greatest degree, in order for the doctrine to be realistic and in tune with human nature. All this is required, as any doctrine worth its salt can not suppress in men and women their deep-rooted propensity towards freedom.

All the above is correct and proper to some extent. Yet, it is a major function of any social doctrine, which attempts to build its structure on solid foundations within the human soul, to take cognisance of the variety of views and tendencies among people and their differing needs, while attempting in the process to accommodate them and find as much common ground as possible. To accept, and cater for, only one major plank of those views/tendencies, and endeavour to satisfy those to the utmost degree possible to the detriment of other views/tendencies, would not be acceptable.

People have an intrinsic leaning towards liberty, due to their natural dislike of coercion and bigotry. At the same time, every person has essential needs, and is prone to certain attitudes/viewpoints. For instance, individuals require some serenity and security in their lives, because worry and turbulence are disturbing and annoying – just like coercion and authoritarianism. When all social guarantees are absent, people would lose a major part of their requirements, and feel deprived of their natural tendency for stability and confidence, exactly as if they have foregone their freedom through the setting up of a totalitarian system which represses and coerces them.

We can therefore stress the primacy of accommodating requisite human needs with people's necessity to be free. Any viable doctrine would be required to balance the normal human propensity for freedom with the essential requirement of confidence and stability, in order for that doctrine to be practical and of service to the public at large. When certain needs and propensities are left to one side, while a focus is placed on one major aspect – as the capitalist doctrine has done – this will clash with the chief doctrinal requirements for practical feasibility.

Finally, it can be asserted that the capitalist rejection of realistic freedom and security is perfectly consistent with capitalist thinking. Such security embodies a limitation on individual liberty, and this would not resonate positively within the context of fundamental capitalist concepts on people and the universe.

Constraints and pressures on liberty may derive their rationale from the current of history, as Marxism maintains in the light of the theory of historical materialism. According to Marxist thinking, the dictatorship of the proletariat delineates people's freedom and applies pressure on members of society, but all this is claimed to be the inevitable consequence of the laws of history. Capitalism, on the other hand, does not believe in historical materialism as it is conceived and sequenced in the special Marxist fashion.

Alternatively, the justification for constraints and pressures may stem from higher authority, as religion insists. Here, the higher power stipulates certain guarantees which limit individual liberty, instituting thereby a specific social path for human life. In its fundamental concepts, capitalism does not accept this, because religion is supposed to be separated from the realities of life.

It may also be suggested that pressure and limitation may emanate form innate human feelings: people sensing the impact of their own conscience calling upon them to adhere to certain moral values, and placing limits on their demeanour and actions towards others. However, within the capitalist context, conscience is essentially a reflection of customs and established mannerism, rather than resulting from some kind of moral philosophy. Put somewhat differently, capitalism would recognise conscience as an external pressure, instead of being an innate factor doing its work from inside.

It can thus be seen that capitalism is incapable of interpreting any pressure/limitation on freedom through historical necessity, religion or conscience. In this connection, the capitalist standpoint is closely linked to its ideological roots, its concepts on the universe and human beings, as well as on history, religion and morals. Al this has furnished the foundations for the political orientation of capitalism on government and various social authorities.

Proponents of capitalism do not see any reasons for these authorities to meddle in areas affecting individual liberty, except in so far as necessary to protect individual freedoms from anarchy or clashes, because this is the extent of intervention allowed by people themselves. Outside these limits, no justification is envisaged for any encroachment on individual liberties, whether claims for such limits rest on historical, religious, moral or behavioural grounds.

All that ideological flow leads capitalism to an emphasis on liberty in the economic sphere, rejecting any rights for the State or other organs to institute guarantees or provide limitations.

Index of Names

Subject Index